Sex,
Lies &
Soul Ties

Sex, Lies & Soul Ties

A Comprehensive Guide to Understanding the
Causes and Effects of Ungodly Soul Ties

Tiffany Buckner

Anointed Fire House

www.anointedfirehouse.com

Sex, Lies and Soul Ties
Copyright © 2015
Author Tiffany Buckner
Email: info@anointedfire.com
Publisher: Anointed Fire™ House
Publisher's Website: www.anointedfirehouse.com

ISBN-10: 0692522662
ISBN-13: 978-0692522660

Disclaimer: This book is designed to provide information and motivation to our readers. It is sold with the understanding that the publisher is not engaged to render any type of psychological, legal, or any other kind of professional advice. No warranties or guarantees are expressed or implied by the author, since every man has his own measure of faith. The individual author(s) shall not be liable for any physical, psychological, emotional, financial, or commercial damages, including; but not limited to, special, incidental, consequential or other damages. Our views and rights are the same: You are responsible for your own choices, actions, and results.

The stories in this book are fictional. Names, characters, businesses, places, events and incidents are either the products of the author's imagination or used in a fictitious manner. Any resemblance to actual persons, living or dead, or actual events is purely coincidental.

Dedication

I dedicate this book to its original Author: YAHWEH. You are the Author and Finisher of my faith, and you have proven yourself to be my everything. I pray that every word in this book glorifies your Almighty name. I give you the glory and the honor for everything you've done and for who you are. Thank you for entrusting me to birth this book.

Your loving daughter and vessel,

Tiffany Buckner

Table of Contents

Introduction/ Warning

I remember logging on to Facebook one day and posting a very powerful message about soul ties. The topic of illegal relationships has become a passion of mine because God is passionate about seeing His people set free of the bondage brought on by sexual sin. Five minutes after I posted the status, I came across the status of a young woman whom I had recently (and regretfully) added to my friend's list. She had just posted her take on the soul tie debate (via her page, of course). In her post, she attempted to dispute the validity of the soul tie theory. She kept talking about *her feelings* about the topic of soul ties and why *she didn't think* soul ties were real. Now, I can't exactly say that she posted her status as a passive-aggressive way of responding to my status because I try not to think along those lines since social media is just social media. Nevertheless, what I could say was that we were speaking on the same subject at the same time, but drawing different conclusions. Of course, most people didn't agree with her because they have enough understanding about soul ties to know that they are real. One person did agree with her, however, and that wasn't surprising to me because I'd seen that same person standing in agreement with other ungodly doctrines and behaviors in the past. I knew that both women were likely babes in Christ; they were both women who tried many times to bend and shape the Word of God to fit their own personal molds, and this is something commonly done by babes in Christ. They were women who didn't want to make any more changes to their personal lives. Instead, they found doctrines that would allow them to remain as they were: soul tied, unforgiving and unrepentant. Of course, God does not conform to our sinful nature. We have to be transformed by the renewing of our minds.

I brushed off their behaviors, nevertheless, my spirit man was bothered because there are so many people who will never truly know Christ. Many people will come to the knowledge of Christ, but never know the reality of Him, meaning, they'll know that He's real, and they'll know many stories about Him, but they will never personally or intimately know Him. Several of these people have gone on to become ministers of the gospel, but instead of preaching the good news, they will mislead and shatter some of the broken souls who come their way. They will become leaders who preach by emotion, never taking the time to study and show themselves approved. In their blindness, they will lead many people into captivity, and from there, they'll tell them to "keep on praying" because "God's not finished with them yet."

I didn't respond to the young lady's status because she wasn't asking if soul ties were real; she'd taken it upon herself to tell people that they weren't real because "they didn't make sense to her." Her position was that she wanted more proof. The problem is whenever you accept a doctrine as true, you will begin to teach that doctrine. Many people don't study the Word and conduct the necessary research; instead, they lean to their own understanding and draw a conclusion from there. They then begin to teach the false doctrines they've accepted, and they try to reason using human intellect, rather than the Word of God. Others start ministries where they feed their followers the doctrines they were once fed, meaning, they don't seek the truth for themselves. Instead, they go to theology school or join someone's church, and from there, they take what they're told, start a church, and feed those doctrines to their followers. Some of those followers then become leaders and do the same.

The sad part is... the young lady who spoke against soul ties is not alone. There are many leaders today who refuse to teach on the subject of soul ties because they are currently soul tied themselves. Additionally, when studying about sex and soul ties in the Word of God, what you'll find is that the whole truth is rarely taught. The reason for this is that we were taught that fornication is premarital sex and we were taught that marriage occurred at the altar or the courthouse, but these are only fractions of the truth.

As you continue on in this guide, you will learn the truth about soul ties and you will learn how to be set free from them. There is a lot of information in this book that you might not be able to chew (today), but if you pray about it and conduct the necessary research, I'm confident that God will reveal the truth to you.

Soul Tied and Broken

You lift up your weeping eyes in the wee hours of the morning. Another day has passed, but you're still stuck in yesterday. How is it that someone you've loved so much could behave so wickedly towards you? An unfamiliar and uneasy queasiness comes over you. You rub your belly, wondering why your stomach feels the way it does. You dance with the idea that after all that happened, you'd managed to conceive a child from the man you're now angrily referring to as your ex. What if you are pregnant? How bittersweet would that be? Hope takes the place of sound reasoning in your mind. You tell yourself that if you are pregnant, your ex will be forced to deal with the situation that drove the two of you apart. At the same time, he would be tied to you for life. Since you're still soul tied to him, you smile at the idea of him not being able to sever all ties with you because of an unplanned pregnancy. So you call up your ex to tell him

1

the developing news. You don't want to wait to tell him after you've taken a pregnancy test because you pretty much know you are not pregnant. Nevertheless, you want to see how he would react to the news and you want to stop dealing with the pain and confusion brought on by your recent breakup. After all, you believe him to be a somewhat decent guy; he's just not that great with touchy-feely conversations, but being pregnant just might make him a little more empathetic towards you.

The phone rings and he doesn't answer. Anger and hurt swell in your belly, but you're determined to reach him, so you keep calling until he answers. After listening to him rebuke you about constantly calling his phone, you finally get your chance to speak. "Sorry, I wasn't going to call you, but I just thought you should know I haven't seen my period. I think I'm pregnant. I have an appointment with Dr. Doe's office on Monday, so I'll call and let you know the results. I'm confident that I am pregnant because I've never missed my period before, so I wanted to tell you first, but again, my appointment is on Monday." Suddenly, the line is eerily silent. Did he hang up the phone? "Are you still there?" you ask. He humbly confirms that he's still on the line. *Finally!* His tone has changed towards you. Sure, he's just spoken a few words, but for the first time since you've broken up, he's not yelling at you.

"Are you sure?"

"Am I sure of what?"

"That you're pregnant?"

"Oh. Yes, I think I am. I've been feeling sick lately and my menstruation was supposed to come three weeks ago, but it didn't. Like I told you before, I've never missed my period."

Note: You're lying. Your period is only a few days behind, but you don't want him to know that because he'd see how desperate you've become.

After speaking with your ex, you hang up the phone feeling relieved, excited and hopeful. Maybe... just maybe, he sees you in a different light now. Maybe... just maybe, he wants to right his wrongs, and the two of you can reconcile. You hang on to your newfound (and unstable) thread of hope, and fear takes the place of anger. Now, you're hoping against all hope that you are pregnant, but deep down inside, you know that you're not, so you keep avoiding taking a pregnancy test. Monday comes, and even though you didn't have a doctor's appointment, you know that you have to tell your ex something about your condition; plus, your menstruation came on Saturday. What's a girl to do? Some women would tell the guy that it was just a pregnancy scare; other women would pretend to be pregnant, and then, claim to have had a miscarriage. The most wicked of them all would lie to their guys and say that they'd miscarried because of the stress brought on by the recent breakup. Many would try to seduce the guy back into the bedroom, where they'd tirelessly try to get pregnant. The majority of these women would develop an anger towards their estranged lovers when they realize that they're truly, without a shadow of a doubt, being rejected by them. The few who do turn out to be pregnant would be bitter towards their child's father, and that bitterness would determine how they raise their child or children with the guy. The point is... ungodly soul ties may look different when being worn by various women, but the pain is all the same.

A lot of women try to sex their way into loving relationships, and because of this, they often find themselves oversexed, soul tied and lonely. Many come to the reality that their lovers don't truly know their hearts and have never shown genuine interest in getting to know them. The truth is... a person who does not truly know you cannot truly love you, and deep down inside, both men and women know when they aren't truly loved. The problem is... most people repeatedly lie to themselves when they are bound by soul ties. Nevertheless, we serve a faithful God who is determined to get us to see the light of the truth, even when that truth breaks our hearts.

Why would God rather see us alone and brokenhearted than soul tied and happy? Because a broken heart can and will heal over time, but an ungodly soul tie will eventually kill or ruin the lives of everyone who is bound by it. God looks at where He wants us to be and compares it to where we are. He then looks at what's keeping us from getting to where He wants us to be, and all too often, it's the people we've chosen as life partners who are standing in our way. While we are in those relationships, God will oftentimes begin changing our minds, and that's when we find ourselves in conflict with the people we've chosen for ourselves. Conflict is not always the result of an attack from the devil; sometimes, it is the result of us growing up. The more we grow in the Lord, the less compatible we will be to the people we've soul tied ourselves to. That's why God wants us saved, sanctified and filled with the Holy Spirit before He releases our God-appointed spouses to us. Relationships not established by God are scheduled to break apart when the people in them begin to grow apart, but Godly relationships are designed to grow stronger as the people in them grow wiser.

Genesis 2:24: Therefore shall a man leave his father and his mother, and shall cleave unto his wife: and they shall be one flesh.

Cleaving takes time. It doesn't always happen immediately. As a matter of fact, most couples fight because one or both parties involved isn't cleaving to the other. The one who refuses to cleave often accuses the other of being clingy. Ironically, one of the definitions of "cleave" is "to cling". This means that one person wants the benefits of marriage without the responsibilities of marriage, and this inevitably brings about strife in any relationship.

Ungodly soul ties often result in unforgiveness, distrust and confusion. What happens in ungodly soul ties is... one or both parties involved in a relationship will often suffer from a broken heart brought on by being in that relationship, and then, the broken heart brought on by the ending of the relationship. There aren't many things on earth that can compare to the pain associated with being broken up while soul tied. That's why so many men and women are angry, bitter, distrusting, disloyal, unforgiving and ungodly. Many don't realize that even though they live alone, they are married in God's eyes, and their souls know this.

Ungodly soul ties are like debt. When a person is bound by them, they feel like they've been robbed by the people they're soul tied to. A married person feels indebted to the person he or she is married to, and the couple will spend their lives trying to show their appreciation to one another. That's what Godly soul ties do. They help you to realize your value in the Lord, all the while, teaching you to appreciate your spouse, or better yet, make your spouse aware of their value in the Lord. Godly soul ties teach us to be better people. The word "appreciate" means "to increase in value" or "to show the value of" something. In contrast, ungodly soul ties depreciate us; they make us feel worthless. When a person is bound by ungodly soul ties, they feel as if they're owed something because they've given the better part of themselves to someone, hoping to get something in return. When they don't get what they expect, but instead, receive lies and deception, they realize that they can't simply take the better part of themselves away from the people their souls are entangled with. Because of this, they are not morally qualified for the types of men or women who were once attracted to them. Think of it this way. Let's say you had a brand new Lexus that you were trying to sell for a little over forty thousand dollars. Someone comes along and gets that Lexus from you on credit, and for two years, they pay their monthly bill to you without fail. Suddenly, one day, the payments start coming late, and before long, the payments stop coming altogether. You call the lessee of the Lexus, but he isn't answering your calls, and whenever he does answer, he's short, agitated and abrupt with you. One day, you wake up to find that the Lexus he promised to pay off is parked in your driveway and it looks nothing like the bright and shiny car that he initially took away. It's beat up and devalued. The paint isn't as glossy as it once was. As a matter of fact, there are scratches on the car, the windshield is cracked, and the interior of the vehicle looks awful. When you look under the hood, you find that the he did nothing to maintain the vehicle's engine. The radiator needs to be replaced, the cooling fan is on its last spin, one of the gaskets is blown, and the engine is just about ready to give out. Inside the Lexus, you find a note from him, and instead of apologizing for not being faithful and honoring his vow to fully purchase the Lexus, he accuses you of being unfair. He tries to justify his behavior by saying that the car was giving him trouble since the day he drove it off the lot, even though you leased him a near perfect car. Now, it's hard for you to sell that Lexus for its projected book value because he has devalued it, and it's going to take a lot of time and money to restore that vehicle. That's how soul ties work. Someone comes along and promises to take good care of your heart, but of course, they can't afford to call themselves your husband or wife at the moment. They want to lease you for a while, and they want to pay the price for you in small installments. Because they didn't pay the full price for you, they don't know your value, so they don't take good care of you. Like a poorly maintained vehicle, you begin to break down after being used, abused and neglected over a period of time. Instead of realizing that they are the ones putting all of the wear and tear on your heart, they blame you for your condition, and eventually return you to the singles' market. Over the course of your relationship to them, they've wired you to start, but they haven't wired you to go very far because they wanted you to break down and stay in a place where they could easily find you. Now, because you're broken, beat up and devalued, you find yourself being overlooked by decent people. The people who want to romantically link themselves to you want the same terms that your previous lover had; they want to lease you, but they don't want to marry you. With each new soul tie, you find yourself being devalued more and more until the people you once felt were the lowest forms of life on the planet begin to look down on you.

Whenever a human being feels devalued, that person will enter one relationship after another, trying to find someone who appreciates them, but in reality each new soul tie will depreciate

them all the more. That's why you see so many
people who were once innocent, loving and
childlike in relationships with some of today's
most rebellious people. They were broken
down so much until they started believing they
weren't good enough for a decent man or
woman. Anytime you look at a person and
think you're not good enough for that person,
you're more than likely soul tied to someone
who has caused you to feel worthless. Your
past will always come forth and interrupt your
future if you are presently soul tied. At the
same time, even when God has freed you from
ungodly soul ties, you still have to let God
renew your mind so you can see how valuable
you are to Him.

God wants to break every ungodly bond away
from you, but Satan wants to use them to
break you. Satan wants you to devalue yourself
to the point where you accept a less than
desirable life with a person who doesn't know
your full value. If someone doesn't recognize
what you are worth, they won't pay the full
price for your hand in marriage. As a matter of

fact, they will repeatedly devalue you because broken people break people. A broken man does not want his wife to ever realize her value because she may realize that she's better off without him and vice versa. A broken man will oftentimes tell his wife what *he feels* is wrong with her. He wants to demean her until she's so low that he's able to esteem himself as a man who is out of her league; he wants to present himself as her blessing. When a woman thinks she's not good enough for the man she has, she will continually work to earn his affections, and she will tolerate his less than desirable ways. That's why Satan wants you in an ungodly soul tie. He wants to control how you view yourself, and by doing so, he can control you. He can then break you, mold you and form you into the woman he wants you to be. The same goes for men, of course. If you find yourself married to a broken woman, she will do everything in her power to demean, manipulate and break you because she wants to control you. Why do broken women want to control their men? Because they've trusted people in the past who've wrecked their lives

13

and left them for dead. This isn't a justification for their brokenness because they were supposed to go to God and be made whole again before even attempting to enter any new relationships. Instead, they chose to use one man to fix the gaping holes in their souls that were created by other men, but no man has the strength, tools or ability to repair a broken soul. After being broken up from the men they've soul tied themselves to, they decided to control the direction of their relationships by trying to control the men they were in relationships with.

Wanting to be married is good, but being set free from ungodly soul ties is far better. Speak with the Lord about your present condition and let Him heal, deliver and restore you. No man or woman can do God's job for Him. You have to use the Word of God to fix yourself, and then, let Him present you to your spouse. Remember this: The wrong man (or woman) is not a blessing; they are lessons to be learned, and the time you spend with them is the time you will spend learning that lesson.

Let's Talk About Sex

The average person (in and outside the church) sees sex as nothing more than a pleasurable experience between two people or a physical expression of love. With this limited view of sex, it is no wonder that divorce rates are so high. Many believers get married just to have "legal" sex (sex not considered fornication), but when they are tried as spouses, they are found to be unprepared, selfish and perverse. The truth is that God created sex, but He did not do so just to pleasure the flesh; He created it for procreation. One of the perks of sex, however, is that it can be pleasurable to the flesh because it's one of the rewards of marriage. Nevertheless, sex is very much like worship. God requires that we worship Him in Spirit and in Truth, and whenever we do so, our worship experience will be an intimate one. Worship is an expression of our love and gratitude to God, and He takes pleasure in our worship. However, there's more to worship than meets the eye.

The Hebrew word for worship is "shachah", which means "to bow down, reverence". The Greek word for worship is "proskuneo", which, according to Strong's Concordance, means "to kiss the hand to (towards) one, in token of reverence." There are two more Greek words for "worship" and they are "sebomai" and "latreuo". The following definitions are courtesy of Strong's Concordance:

- *Sebomai: to revere, to worship. (Reference: The KJV New Testament Greek Lexicon)*
- *Latreuo: to serve for hire. (Reference: The NAS New Testament Greek Lexicon)*

To worship God means to humble one's self before Him. Worship is not only an expression of our love and gratitude towards God, but worship is only intimate when it's backed by our knowledge of God. That's why John the Evangelist said in John 4:24, "God is a Spirit: and they that worship him must worship him in spirit and in truth."

Worship involves our bodies, souls and our

spirits. First, in worship, we'll either lay our bodies prostrate before God or we will stand and declare His majesty. Our mouths will pour out the content of our hearts (subconscious minds) and declare what we believe. We believe that He is God. We believe that He is worthy of our praises. We believe that there is no other God but Him. We express our beliefs to Him through words or song, and as we worship Him, our spirits will get involved. Our spirits will worship God in His Spirit. This doesn't necessarily mean that we will speak in tongues every time we worship Him, but it means that our spirit man will connect with His Spirit in agreement (if our worship is done in spirit and in truth). To worship God, we are declaring that He is worthy of our praise and worship, but how can we say that He is worthy of our praise if we do not truly know Him? How can we count Him as worthy of our worship if we do not serve Him in the very bodies we are attempting to worship Him in?

To worship God in truth, we are declaring that there is no other God but YAHWEH. We are declaring that Jesus (YESHUA) Christ is Lord. We are declaring that the Word of God is true. To worship Him in truth, we must believe what we're saying, otherwise, our worship isn't for real. For example, some people speak the truth and attempt to worship God, but they have not submitted their hearts to Him. They don't believe in Him entirely, or they may be experimenting with other gods (devils). A person who doesn't have a heart for God cannot truly please Him because their mouths are declaring words that they have no faith in. **Matthew 15:8 (NIV):** These people honor me with their lips, but their hearts are far from me. **Hebrews 11:6:** But without faith it is impossible to please him: for he that cometh to God must believe that he is, and that he is a rewarder of them that diligently seek him.

True worship produces fruit, because not only are you declaring that God is good, but you are humbling yourself before Him. To worship God, we must be on one accord with Him, meaning, we must agree with and obey Him. You'll notice that whenever you truly begin to worship, your spirit man will get involved, and in many cases, you speak in the tongues of angels. This means your spirit man is in one accord with your body and your soul.

Speaking in tongues isn't always planned, but in most cases, spontaneous. Additionally, when we truly worship God, He responds by blessing, healing and restoring us.

2 Chronicles 7:14 (KJV): If my people, which are called by my name, shall humble themselves, and pray, and seek my face, and turn from their wicked ways; then will I hear from heaven, and will forgive their sin, and will heal their land.

How does this relate to sex? Sex is similar to worship. It was designed by God to be an intimate, passionate and fruitful experience between a man and his wife. The primary purpose of it is procreation, but sex shouldn't be a mundane experience. When a man loves his wife and the wife loves her husband, sex is one of the many ways they can express their love for one another. Anytime there's no intimacy in sex, it becomes nothing more than a repetitious and unpleasant ritual. Additionally, sex without (true) knowledge of the person you're having it with is not love, but lust. How so? To truly love someone, you must know that person. That's why many marriages fail today. A lot of people marry individuals they don't truly know, but once they are married, they begin to discover their spouses' (unsexy) flaws. People tend to marry their perception of who a person is or the potential they believe that person has, but they always divorce the reality of who their spouses are.

You'll notice that during sex, the natural position is that the woman (wife) is under her husband. Now, of course, there are many positions that people put themselves in to have sex, but the natural position is called missionary. In the missionary position, the wife lies down and is covered by her husband. This order, in no doubt, represents the order God initiated for our relationships to Him and our spouses.

1 Corinthians 11:3 (ESV): But I want you to understand that the head of every man is

Christ, the head of a wife is her husband, and the head of Christ is God.

Man is the head (covering) of his wife, meaning, he is (supposed to be) the protector and provider for his wife and the children she bears, just as Jesus is the Protector and Provider for His people and the children they bear. When sex is done outside of perversion, it is much more than a gratifying experience to the flesh, but it also strengthens the bond (soul tie) between a man and his wife. When we know God and we seek to please Him, He takes pleasure in us. When we know our spouses (inside and outside of the bedroom), and we seek to please them (inside and outside the bedroom), our sexual experiences with them will serve to strengthen our bonds with them. The stronger the tie, the more pleasurable the sex! That's why couples who've been happily married for decades reportedly have the best sex. They know their spouses both physically and intimately. They've released many of their worries, doubts and fears and they just enjoy one another because they are secure in their marriages. Marriage without security is a fearful and dreadful experience that undoubtedly affects a couple's sex life.

Sex establishes soul ties, and the initial purpose of a soul tie was to ensure that people wouldn't be casual with sex, meaning, it wouldn't be easy for them to sleep with strangers. Soul ties also give us insight to our relationship with God. We are one body with whomever we sleep with, just as we are one Spirit with God whenever we get saved. To be married simply means to be one flesh with someone, and again, marriage is established by sex. People break up when they are one body with their spouses (legal or illegal), but they are not in one accord. When a couple is in one accord, the sexual experience is far greater than those between one thousand perverse people, even if those people had access to every tool, toy and gadget found in the adult stores of today. We must keep in mind that the devil is always trying to mimic God, so a perverse couple cannot and will not truly experience the whole intimate experience that Godly couples enjoy.

That's why they prim, probe and hurt one another trying to get a more heightened sexual encounter.

Sex, between a man and his wife, is far better when there are no lies, misconceptions or fears dividing them. When a couple is in one accord, their souls will not just be tied, but their souls will get intimately involved, agreeing that the two should be one. This means their minds will be free of the fear, doubts and suspicions brought on by deception and sin. When the mind is free to love, people begin to will themselves to relax more, love more and express their love for one another more because there is nothing holding them back. Of course, our emotions then get involved in a good way, and that's why we'll experience a sudden rush of joy. Our souls will then communicate with our bodies, signaling the body to produce a more heightened climatic experience because the mind will tell the body that it does not have to hold back. If you've ever been sexually involved with someone, it is likely that you can relate to feeling like you want to do more, but you can't. You want to express yourself more, but something's holding you back. When this happens, the average couple tries to experiment with different sex positions, and sometimes, even toys because they are trying to pull something out of one another that can only be released when their souls and bodies are on one accord. This leads the couple to becoming even more perverse because the body has limitations, therefore, the couple has to learn to stimulate or psych their minds into triggering a more heightened orgasm. More and more, people invite pain, fear, and other people into their bedrooms in their attempts to satisfy a growing and unquenchable lust. After all, lust has the belly of hell; it can never be satisfied. It can only be momentarily appeased when it's being entertained.

As people grow more and more perverse, they begin to become sexual daredevils, often trying to explore ways to reach new heights of pleasure. After a while, one sexual partner is not enough; the perverse couple will find themselves lusting after other people. This lust is the result of sexual curiosity. Some people will venture out and have adulterous affairs in their attempts to satisfy the growing monster within. Others will remain faithful to their spouses, but they will oftentimes become more deviant in the bedroom. That's why some people like to be spanked, pinched, choked, bitten, or cursed at. Such souls are perverted and looking for ways to trigger a response from their brains. You see, the brain understands sex and will cause the body to perform the repetitious behaviors of sexual intercourse, but the brain is limited to what it knows. Perverted souls like to experiment with words and actions because they are attempting to get a different response from their brains. Some people like to experiment with adrenaline. During sex, the body releases adrenaline from its adrenal glands. Google's Online Dictionary defines "adrenaline" as:

- *a hormone secreted by the adrenal glands, especially in conditions of stress, increasing rates of blood circulation, breathing, and carbohydrate*

*metabolism and preparing muscles for
exertion.*

Even though the body releases adrenaline
during sex, perverted souls will often attempt
to get the body to release more adrenaline by
inviting pain into their sexual experiences.
That's because adrenaline can cause us to
momentarily not feel any pain. Adrenaline is
like a drug, and when it is released, we
experience increased heart rates, heightened
senses, increased breathing and a sudden
boost of energy. Some people invite fear,
which, of course, is a spirit into their bedrooms.
A good example is a couple who likes to "play
rape", whereas, the man pretends to be a thief
or a sexual predator. The woman pretends to
be the victim, and instead of voluntarily
submitting to sexual intercourse, she pretends
to resist her lover. The lover then uses his
strength to overpower her, and he mimics
many of the behaviors associated with an
actual rape. He may cover her mouth, rip her
clothes, physically bind her with ropes or
handcuffs, and in some more sadistic cases, he

may choke or abuse her. In many of these instances, the man swears or curses at his female partner. That's because cursing has been found to release endorphins in the brain, and endorphins are responsible for relieving pain and stress. Additionally, endorphins lead to feelings of euphoria. For the couple, this creates a cocktail of hormones as it increases the adrenaline flowing through their brains, and signals the body to release dopamine. According to psychologytoday.com, dopamine is:

- *A neurotransmitter that helps control the brain's reward and pleasure centers. Dopamine also helps regulate movement and emotional responses, and it enables us not only to see rewards, but to take action to move toward them. Dopamine deficiency results in Parkinson's Disease, and people with low dopamine activity may be more prone to addiction. The presence of a certain kind of dopamine receptor is also associated with sensation-seeking people, more commonly known as "risk takers."*

Perversion leads people to become creative in their attempts to experience what they perceive to be heightened sexual encounters. Now, the orgasms experienced by perverse couples aren't necessarily good orgasms. In most cases, it is the combination of fear, pain and the pleasures of an orgasm that makes the experience more memorable. This means people tend to seek uncommon sexual encounters, and they label those encounters as good because the encounters were unlike any others they've experienced. Nevertheless, when the soul agrees with the spirit and the two work together to communicate with the body, the body automatically responds with pleasure, especially when the couple is on one accord. In layman's terms, a perverse couple has to work harder, manipulate their bodies more and psych their minds in their attempts to reach heights of orgasm that righteous couples effortlessly enjoy every day.

Let's face it. Sex is a pleasurable experience and

most of us like it. Nevertheless, sex outside of marriage God's way is not only illegal, but it's not fulfilling. People who engage themselves in fornication often find their souls tied to people who want their bodies, but want nothing to do with their minds. They find themselves soul tied to people who want to spend a season or two with them, but not a lifetime. A woman, for example, who allows her body to be used by a man for fornication will almost always find herself becoming that man's guilty pleasure. He won't desire a lifetime with her. He won't desire to know her intimately outside of the bedroom. Please know that intimacy begins with our words and actions and flows inside of the bedroom. He won't seek the full knowledge of her, meaning, even if she had five thousand sexual encounters with that man, she will never experience the overwhelming, overpowering, mind-changing satisfaction that she would have experienced had she waited on her God-ordained husband. Additionally, her illegal partner won't reach his greatest peak, but because the body will tell him that there are sexual heights he has yet to explore, he will aimlessly experiment with (abuse) his partner's body. His body will want a greater sexual experience with his partner, but his partner's soul will desire a greater connection with him. That's because women aren't always led by the lusts of their flesh, but are instead, often led by their desires to be loved.

A woman's makeup makes it impossible for her to have pointless and emotionless sex, although many women have hardened their hearts and will easily submit their bodies to multiple men in a year, month or a day. For example, a prostitute's heart is hardened by the sin she's in and the hurts she's endured. This doesn't mean that sex no longer affects her, because it does. It simply means she's learned to emotionally disconnect herself from her body. She doesn't think love will be birthed through her many fornications. She doesn't expect the men she's lying with to love her. She sleeps with men while having a "no strings attached" attitude, nevertheless, she becomes one person with every man who's lain with her. **1 Corinthians 6:15-16 (NIV):** Do you not know that your bodies are members of Christ himself? Shall I then take the members of Christ and unite them with a prostitute? Never! Do you not know that he who unites himself with a prostitute is one with her in body? For it is said, "The two will become one flesh."

The two will become one flesh; we get that, but did you know that the average church thinks this only relates to legal marital unions? This is not so! When God said, "the two shall become one flesh," He was speaking of the coming together of a man and his wife, but this coming together didn't happen when the couple said "I do" in front of their pastors. This coming together happened the very moment they had sex!

Genesis 24:63-67 (ESV): And Isaac went out to meditate in the field toward evening. And he lifted up his eyes and saw, and behold, there were camels coming. And Rebekah lifted up her eyes, and when she saw Isaac, she dismounted from the camel and said to the servant, "Who is that man, walking in the field to meet us?" The servant said, "It is my master."

So she took her veil and covered herself. And the servant told Isaac all the things that he had done. Then Isaac brought her into the tent of Sarah his mother and took Rebekah, and she became his wife, and he loved her. So Isaac was comforted after his mother's death.

Isaac took Rebekah into his tent (residency) and she became his wife through sex. Isaac and Rebekah never exchanged vows; they hadn't even met before their "wedding" day. If you remember the story, Abraham (Isaac's father) sent his servant to Mesopotamia to find a wife for his son, Isaac. When the servant arrived in Mesopotamia, he prayed and asked God to choose Isaac's wife, and then, to give him confirmation as to who she was. The servant asked for a sign. He went near the wells of the city and had his camels to kneel down to rest. He said to God that he intended to ask some of the women to draw water from the wells for himself. Whichever woman obliged him, and offered to give water to his camels as well, would be the appointed woman for Isaac. Her offer to give water to his camels was the sign he'd requested from God. As it turned out, Rebekah was that woman. The story goes on to tell us that the servant questioned Rebekah about her family, and when he found out that they were related to Abraham's family, he knew that God had answered his prayers. Rebekah invited him back to her father's house, the servant told the father about Abraham's request, and the father released Rebekah to go back with the servant to become Isaac's wife. When Rebekah saw Isaac, she covered her face with her veil. Now, many people think that it was customary for the women of that day to wear veils, but it was not. Rebekah didn't wear her veil in the presence of Eliezer, the servant. She covered her face at the sight of Isaac. Many theologians believe this was a ceremonial practice where the virgin would veil herself before she came together with her groom. Her husband-to-be would then uncover her before the two became one person. Nevertheless, Jewish women did not walk around wearing veils; only prostitutes covered their faces to hide their identities. That's why Tamar covered her face with a veil when she saw Judah, her father-in-law, approaching (see Genesis 38:14).

Another story to look at is the story of Jacob, Rachel and Leah. Jacob fell in love with Rachel and asked Laban, Rachel's father, for her hand in marriage. In exchange for Rachel, Jacob agreed to be Laban's servant for seven years, but Laban deceived him and gave him Leah instead.

Genesis 29:15-30 (ESV): Then Laban said to Jacob, "Because you are my kinsman, should you therefore serve me for nothing? Tell me, what shall your wages be?" Now Laban had two daughters. The name of the older was Leah, and the name of the younger was Rachel. Leah's eyes were weak, but Rachel was beautiful in form and appearance. Jacob loved Rachel. And he said, "I will serve you seven years for your younger daughter Rachel." Laban said, "It is better that I give her to you than that I should give her to any other man; stay with me." So Jacob served seven years for Rachel, and they seemed to him but a few days because of the love he had for her.

Then Jacob said to Laban, "Give me my wife

that I may go in to her, for my time is completed." So Laban gathered together all the people of the place and made a feast. But in the evening he took his daughter Leah and brought her to Jacob, and he went in to her. (Laban gave his female servant Zilpah to his daughter Leah to be her servant.) And in the morning, behold, it was Leah! And Jacob said to Laban, "What is this you have done to me? Did I not serve with you for Rachel? Why then have you deceived me?" Laban said, "It is not so done in our country, to give the younger before the firstborn. Complete the week of this one, and we will give you the other also in return for serving me another seven years." Jacob did so, and completed her week. Then Laban gave him his daughter Rachel to be his wife. (Laban gave his female servant Bilhah to his daughter Rachel to be her servant.) So Jacob went in to Rachel also, and he loved Rachel more than Leah, and served Laban for another seven years.

Again, we come to see how marriage was viewed and how marriage is established. On the day that Jacob was supposed to marry Rachel, Laban threw a party to celebrate the impending union. This was customary Jewish tradition. Jacob was likely intoxicated when he slept with Leah. Nevertheless, because he'd slept with her, Leah had become his wife and his responsibility. If you continue to read the story in the Bible, you'll see that Jacob continued on as Leah's husband, even though he eventually married Rachel. Jacob ended up having six sons and a daughter with Leah.

There were no exchanging of vows between Jacob and Leah, nor were vows exchanged between Jacob and Rachel. Jacob and Laban simply made a deal, and the marriages between Jacob and both of Laban's daughters were established in the dark of the night. The point here is... there is no such thing as premarital sex, since marriage is established the moment sex happens between two people. Marriage is considered legal when:

1. The woman is a virgin or a widow.
2. The man agrees before God and two or three witnesses to cover (provide and

protect) the woman he's desiring to join himself to for the rest of his life.

Nowadays, women aren't being given away by their fathers anymore, but are instead, empowered to choose their own husbands. (Note: Nowadays, fathers traditionally walk their daughters down the aisle and "give them away" to the grooms, even if they do not agree with the unions. This means that society has changed the "giving away of the bride" to nothing more than a cultural practice). The woman is required to love, honor, remain faithful to and respect her husband all the days of his life. I know this may sound barbaric, especially since we have so many feminine movements nowadays, but the truth is... the prerequisite of marital laws were designed to protect women! How so? God gave man the position as head of his home, meaning, men possess an authority that women do not have. Sometimes, a person with authority can and will abuse that power. Sometimes, people want the benefits of marriage without the responsibilities of providing for and protecting their wives. Since marriage is established through sex, plus, Jewish law dictated that a woman who was sexually active was not available for marriage, a law was needed to keep men from marrying women through the act of sex, and then, leaving them at their fathers' houses. Such an act (in the biblical days) would have brought shame upon that woman's family and the woman in question would be stoned to death. So again, the order established by God was designed to protect women, but, of course, many ungodly men of the past and present day changed how the majority of today's women view submission because they abused their power.

Nowadays, fornication is the norm. The word "fornication" does not mean "premarital sex". The truth is that what we call premarital sex is basically illegal sex, meaning, it is sex performed outside of covenant. It's pretty much test driving a body without committing to it. The Hebrew word for "fornication" is "porneia", which means sexual immorality. Of course, the word "porneia" is where the word "pornography" is derived. Fornication is not just limited to illegal sex (sex outside of covenant); fornication includes adultery, incest, homosexuality and any other form of sexual immorality. Somehow, the church has attempted to redefine fornication, and by doing so, they've released an infectious mindset into this land we call America. Nowadays, a lot of illegally married people find themselves at the altar, preparing to marry other illegally married people, and of course, these marriages were doomed from the start.

Some time ago, I shared my testimony in one of my blogs about having been married twice. As is customary, some uniformed, religious fruitcake came onto my blog and told me to repent. Of course, he was one of the souls who believed that a person could never remarry after having been divorced. I didn't correct him because some explanations require in depth study and a teachable spirit, and it was clear to me that he wasn't looking to learn anything. He simply wanted to express his beliefs. I knew that I would have to go backward and forward with him, laying out line upon line and precept upon precept. By the time I would have been done going backward and forward with him, I would've written a book that he wasn't willing to read. Basically, I'd have to do his work for him. God told us to study and show ourselves approved. I took it upon myself to delete his comment, nevertheless, it reminded me that the church needed to better understand the definition of marriage. What he, and so many other legalistic Christians don't understand is that if we weren't virgins when we stood at the altar (or courthouse) to marry some man or woman, we were already married to every person we'd ever slept with! Now, when I was in the world, I was promiscuous, which means, I had several husbands. When I went to the courthouse in Little Rock, Arkansas to get legally married to the man who would come to be known as my first husband, I was not free to marry and neither was he. When I went to the courthouse in Maribo, Denmark to marry the man who would come to be known as my second husband, I was not free to marry and neither was he. This means our marriages were

40

doomed from the start because we tried to cleave to one another while being soul tied to other people. Simply put, there were just too many people in our bedroom! That's why I can't blame them totally for the failure of those circuses we called marriages. We couldn't cleave, and any time people cannot cleave to one another... they fight! It goes without saying, however, that we serve a merciful, forgiving and loving God, and He can and will free us from every illegal and legal soul tie we've entered if we truly repent. Nevertheless, until we have been freed, we are not free to marry. Sure, we can legally marry people and our marriages will be recognized in the eyes of the law, but in God's eyes, our marriages would be illegal, and therefore, labeled as adultery. Now, please understand that the word "adultery" doesn't mean a married person is sexually engaging with an unmarried or another married person. Adultery, in the Bible, was mostly used in reference to women. Men were only guilty of committing adultery if they abandoned their wives and married other women. You'll notice that Abraham, David and many other great men had multiple wives, and they were never labeled adulterers. That's because there was no commandment in Mosaic Law that prohibited a man from marrying multiple women. The sin was in a man leaving one of his wives if she was not guilty of joining herself to another man. Of course, nowadays, we're no longer living under Mosaic Law (thank God), and God has clarified to us that from the beginning, His design for marriage involved one man and one woman. Abraham, David, Solomon and the many other men of God who practiced polygamy were not punished because there were no laws prohibiting them from marrying multiple women. Nevertheless, they all knew that it was against Jewish customs for them to sleep with women, and then, refuse to provide for and protect those women. That's why Abraham didn't want to put Hagar out when Sarah requested that he do so. It goes without saying that Abraham didn't want to put his son, Ishmael, out and he could have easily put Hagar out without doing the same to Ishmael; after all, the customs of that day allowed concubines to provide children for their barren mistresses. As such, Ishmael was once considered to be Sarah's son; that was, until Sarah had Isaac.

Again, the point is... marriage (in God's eyes) happens the moment sex happens. The law has its own definition of marriage, and this definition is undoubtedly a response to the decreasing popularity of the truth. However, the truth must be told so that the people of God can stop perishing from a lack of knowledge. God said we must study and show ourselves approved, but today's church isn't doing this. Instead, many churches today try to avoid the stigma associated with preaching a message that's foreign to the people's ears. People need to know what sex is as well as its purpose, otherwise, they will become casual lovers, loaning themselves to sin until that sin takes them into bondage.

The purpose of sex is procreation, but the benefits of sex are physical stimulation, pleasure, orgasm and a greater bond with our spouses. There are many health benefits to sex as well. Nevertheless, the main purpose of sex is for a man and a woman to produce after their own kind. Everything God creates is supposed to produce something. Anything that is fruitless is barren, and therefore, accursed.

Soul Tied Saints

There is a difference between a slave and a servant. A slave works for no pay and is forced to work for his master. A servant is paid, but a servant can choose whether he wants to work or not. A servant can quit his job, but a slave cannot quit.

I was once unsaved and addicted to sex. Honestly, I hid my addiction well. I had a meek voice, a soft demeanor, and I came off as super submissive, but I was nowhere near submissive. I answered every older person with respect, referring to older women as "ma'am" and older men as "sir". I wore a smile almost all of the time because I didn't want people to know the devils I was struggling with. With young men, on the other hand, I was sassy, feisty, and sometimes, candid. Most people thought I was a sweet, little shy girl who couldn't hurt a fly, but they were oh-so-wrong. Underneath my mask was a woman picked apart by life, tormented by devils and enslaved to sex. Nevertheless, I didn't want to wear the "whore" label, so I devised a plan to retain my honor. After a few breakups, reality set in. Entering a long term relationship that led to marriage was nowhere in my near future because I wasn't satisfied with the type of men I kept attracting. (Of course, they were all reflections of myself... but I didn't know that back then).

I was soul tied to the men I'd given myself to, and my soul hungered for a covering because it recognized that it was bound, but uncovered. My flesh proved itself to be an enemy of mine because it would not listen to me; it didn't care that I was broken and needed time to find myself. It did not care that I wanted to stop sex cold turkey and just focus on myself. The flesh was busy being the flesh.

Additionally, I felt like my mind had two steering wheels. I was always trying to find my way back to a stable and lighted path, but some dark force kept driving me back to the sin I'd enslaved myself to. To get a handle on myself, I formulated and executed a plan to be sexually monogamous with one guy, while keeping my dating life open. (Yep, it was as stupid as it sounds). I'd met a guy who I could tell was not the monogamous type. He was handsome, successful and everything I thought I wanted in a man, nevertheless, I looked in his eyes and saw something familiar. I saw the same devils in him that I was wrestling him. He was in no way the marrying type, so I knew I couldn't allow him anywhere near my heart. He was addicted to sex and I could see that. I didn't waste any time with him. It was somewhere between eight and ten o'clock one evening when he decided to visit me. We were sitting in his car just talking about life in general. If I remember correctly, he mentioned having gone through a recent divorce and he said that he wasn't sure if he was ready for anything serious just yet. He simply wanted to "see where things went." Ordinarily, if a man had said anything along those lines to me, I would've unleashed a fury of hateful words at him and told him to forget my number, but I saw a perfect opportunity in him. I saw an incredibly handsome man and thought to myself that he would make the perfect bedroom buddy.

We continued to talk, and I could tell he was trying to lead me into believing that there was some type of possible future in store for us, but I wasn't buying it. He was saying what he thought I wanted to hear, but I believed what I could see in his eyes. He just didn't look (or sound) like the marrying type and I wasn't about to let him anywhere near my heart. Every time he looked at me, I could see lust in his eyes, and the monster in him looked to be just as big or even greater than the giant that had been tormenting me. I knew what he wanted, and he appeared to be the perfect guy for what I wanted. I said something along the lines of, "Look, I know you're not the faithful type. I don't want a relationship with you. I just want to have sex with you." I don't remember how long it took him to close his mouth, but I didn't stop there. I explained to him that I wanted a serious relationship, but after being on the dating market, I'd come to see that I'd have to kiss a whole lot of frogs to find my Prince Charming. I told him that I did not want to be a "ho", so I wanted to find one man to sleep with until I met Mr. Right. (I was so lost). My plan was to stop calling and seeing my bedroom buddy if I found myself in a serious relationship. After all, I was rarely in a relationship that I considered serious, but my body didn't care about that. My goal was to not end up in bed with every man who called me his "girlfriend". There was a fiery giant growing inside me, and I'd realized that it was getting out of control. I was trying desperately to find a way to contain it, and my plan seemed like the perfect arrangement to finally bring down my inner Goliath. Of course, the guy agreed to my plan with no hesitation, and for about three years, I tried to convince myself that he was my toy. The reality was we were both Satan's toys.

I was truly a slave to the sin I was bound by, and I was a misinformed slave. Having an all-access pass to my bedroom buddy did not quench those growing desires in me. I found myself calling him whenever my demons woke up. We had kindred spirits... literally. We didn't waste our time with small talk. Our phone calls were oftentimes less than thirty seconds in length. I'd call him and identify myself, and he'd ask me if I wanted to come over. After I confirmed what he already knew, we would then hang up and I'd head over to his house... end of story. What I didn't know was that lust cannot be tamed, try as you may. Anything you feed will grow bigger and stronger until it overtakes you, but whatever you starve will eventually weaken and die. I was feeding the monster within, and it was growing up to be an ugly, inconsolable baby.

Whenever a person is a slave of sin, they will consciously and subconsciously work towards appeasing the sin they are in, and just like I did, a person who's pretty much embraced their sin will try to find glamorous ways to justify their behaviors. For example, many women today say they are just like men when they're not. Not only are they lying to others, but they are deceiving themselves. They fit the very definition of a slave. They say they engage in sexual activity with no strings attached, but the truth is... a slave never expects to receive any wages. A slave will take whatever his or her master gives to or throws at him or her. People often say things out of pride, and many times, they have convinced themselves of the lies they are attempting to sell to others. I was one of them. The truth is, God did not create women to be able to sustain casual sexual intercourse. Every sexual encounter affects us in one way or another! This includes sex with men we are not attracted to in the least bit. Every time a woman lies down with a man, she humbles herself, meaning, she lowers herself. When she's legally married, she humbles herself to her husband, and he then exalts her as his wife. When she's illegally married, she humbles herself before men, and they humiliate her by refusing to acknowledge her as a woman of importance in their lives. Instead, they treat her as a concubine, or even worse, a prostitute.

Characteristics of a Soul Tied, Sex Slave

1. Unforgiveness- Any and every time a person is in unforgiveness, that person

is still bound by soul ties. Unforgiveness is easily discerned or witnessed; for example, if you're courting a woman who has children, and she finds any and every reason to be mad at the father of her children, chances are, she's still soul tied to him.

2. Competitiveness- Anytime you see competitiveness, especially in the romantic arena, you are watching a soul tie in action.

3. Sexual Addiction- When the soul is bound by soul ties, the body will respond to those soul ties by requesting more souls. People with sexual addiction tend to be promiscuous. Some try to combat their promiscuity by entering relationships that have no other purpose but sex, while others simply give in to the insatiable appetite of their flesh. These people are likely in need of demonic deliverance, and are definitely soul tied.

4. An Untamed Libido- Do you find yourself always burning with desire to

the point where you've considered fornication or masturbation? Some would say you have a healthy libido, but the truth is... if you can't get a handle on your cravings, it may be because you are soul tied to someone, and your soul remembers how they made you feel.

5. Sadistic Bedroom Behaviors- When a person behaves sadistically in the bedroom, it's because they are soul tied and looking for new heights of sexual pleasure. Sometimes, they are looking for people to compete with the men or women they've lain with, people they considered great lovers.

6. Sexual Curiosity- Soul tied people often find themselves wanting to try out new things, and sometimes, new people because they aren't exactly satisfied with the people in their lives. Now, don't get me wrong, it's normal to want to try new positions, but a soul tied person's curiosity goes beyond this. They often find themselves desiring to sleep with other people, engage in sadistic sexual

behavior or experiment with sex toys. Of course, this too is oftentimes an issue where deliverance is needed, nonetheless, the person also needs to be set free from soul ties.

7. Distrust- A person who's still soul-tied to someone else will have trouble trusting others because of their past experiences, especially anyone they are romantically linked to.

8. Low Self Esteem-Low self-esteem is almost always the result of a failed relationship, coupled with an unsevered soul tie. It goes without saying that not everyone who has low self-esteem is soul tied to someone.

9. Depression- Depression is oftentimes found in people with unsevered soul ties, however, not everyone who has depression is soul tied to someone else.

10. A "No Strings Attached" Attitude: Anytime you come across someone who can offer themselves up freely, that person is without a shadow of a doubt soul tied to someone else. Honestly,

whenever people become that casual
with their bodies, they are oftentimes
soul tied to many people.
11. Relationship Instability- Soul tied people
are oftentimes unstable in relationships.
This is because they are still married to
others and haven't quite gotten past the
hurts and the betrayals they've endured
in their past relationships.

Of course, there are many more signs that the
person you're engaging with is soul tied to
someone else, but the right thing to do
(always) is to pray about everyone who
attempts to enter your life. Additionally, after
you pray about people, don't tell them who
they are to you or vice versa; let God show you
who they are before you open your mouth and
hand them a label.

A slave of sex isn't the glamorous, seductive
character Hollywood has made her (or him) out
to be. Instead, anyone who struggles with
sexual addiction has a tortured and not-so-
pretty soul. They will oftentimes try to mask the

conditions of their souls by any means necessary.

The topic of sex is still taboo, so many people in the church are embarrassed to talk about anything dealing with their sex lives, including the fact that they need to be set free from the bondage of lust and sexual immorality. They think that if they go to the church long enough, they will wake up one day delivered. Of course, God can touch, heal and restore them while they are seated in the congregation, but more often than not, God requires that we confess our sins and shortcomings before He delivers us.

Because many churches aren't teaching about sex, there are many Christians who believe themselves to be single. These believers call heaven, repeatedly asking to meet their God-appointed spouses, but as the years pass by, they find themselves wondering why their prayers have yet to be answered. The truth is they are already married and have not truly repented of their fornication. When we call

upon the name of the Lord and ask Him for
something, He looks at the condition of our
hearts. If our hearts are not in the condition to
receive anything from Him, He will oftentimes
hand us a mirror so that we can see it for
ourselves. These mirrors sometimes come in
the forms of trials and tribulations. It is when
we are tried that whatever we have in our
hearts will begin to flow out like rivers without
dams. When we see evil pouring out of us, we
should take our hearts to God and confess
what we've found in them. After this, we are to
repent of our sins, which, of course, means to
turn away from those sins. We must then
endure the mind-renewing process where God
changes our minds and gives us new hearts.
This process can be short or lengthy,
depending on our willingness to let God finish
the works in us that He has started. Finally, we
must sow the necessary seeds and let the
seasons play out. Everything underneath the
sun operates in seed-time and harvest. It goes
without saying that most people abort the
process and remain married to their estranged
lovers for years, and sometimes decades. This

undoubtedly keeps them from being found by or finding their God-ordained spouses; after all, anyone who God gives away to be a spouse must first be a blessing. God will not hand an unavailable soul to an available person.

I can't tell you how many times I've received emails from men and women (mostly women) who were complaining about how lengthy their waits have been. I've had women tell me they've been waiting for five plus years to be found by their God-appointed husbands. They have remained abstinent and they have done everything they thought they needed to do to get God to move on their behalves. Eventually, the truth comes out, but they can't seem to see it. Many of them are still soul tied to someone else. Some of the things people say that are telltale signs that they are currently in soul ties with other people include, but are not limited to the following:

1. **My ex got married and I don't think that's fair! I looked on his Facebook page yesterday and saw that he was getting married-** Why are you still

communicating or keeping up with the ex if you don't share any children together?

2. **He cheated on me with some gargoyle-looking woman-** If you are still speaking evil of the woman (or women) your ex cheated on you with or the woman your ex is currently with, you are still soul tied to him; plus, you're still in unforgiveness.

3. **My ex looks horrible now! She's getting back everything she's done to me-** If you're still speaking evil of your ex, it's because you have not yet forgiven her, and you are currently still soul tied to her.

4. **I still talk to my ex's mom because she and I are cool! Sure, I don't have children with her daughter, but I like her and I'm not going to turn my back on her just because her daughter and I aren't together anymore-** Face it. You're still tied to her and trying to keep up with her movements. You can find creative ways to justify your behaviors,

but God will never send your appointed wife into a situation where she's guaranteed to get her heart broken.

5. **I can't stop masturbating-**
Masturbation is oftentimes a sign that you're still bound by a soul tie, nevertheless, it could simply mean that you have been entertaining the lusts of your flesh for so long that your flesh has now overtaken you. Additionally, it can mean you need deliverance from the spirit of perversion.

Soul tied saints often remain bound for years because they don't realize they are still married to someone else. As a matter of fact, many of them don't realize that they are married... period! Many believers don't actually believe in soul ties, and therefore, they remain bound by them. I've come across one or two women so far, who have admitted to not believing in soul ties. What I can recall about one woman in particular is that she's been "waiting" on her God-appointed husband to find her for more than ten years. It goes without saying that she's delayed her own wait because she has not yet repented of her past encounters and asked God to set her free from any and every soul tie she's bound by. The other woman hasn't forgiven her ex, and therefore, is still in bondage to him.

James 4:2-3 (KJV): Ye lust, and have not: ye kill, and desire to have, and cannot obtain: ye fight and war, <u>yet ye have not, because ye ask not</u>.

Many soul tied saints try to praise their way out of sexual bondage, but God desires that we get and remain free. God is willing to set us free if we want to be free, but a person without understanding will almost always return to bondage. That's because they don't know or understand what's been binding them, how it's been binding them and what they need to do to free themselves. The problem is we don't like to come outside our comfort zones, and new information (knowledge) requires that we learn the uncomfortable truth. This would put us in the awkward position of having to take what we've learned and decide whether we want to return to our comfortable bondage or not. Because of this, many believers try to make God meet them in their current mindsets and conditions, rather than them meeting God in His Word so that He could renew their minds and change their conditions. They find churches that encourage them to remain the same, and from there, they offer up repetitious chants before God, asking Him to send them the spouses they've longed for. Nevertheless, God responds by showing them that they are still in bondage. He wants them to repent so He could deliver, restore and heal them, however, they don't think repentance is necessary since they are already in a religious setting. They think to themselves, "How can God use me if I'm not already free?" They harden their hearts to the voice of God and declare their own righteousness. They perform the religious acts of worship, without having a heart of worship. They weary themselves by watching everyone around them who's getting married, especially the people they believe aren't worthy of marriage. They would rather call God unjust or unfair than change their own wicked ways. They preach from the surface of knowledge, but they have no depth of wisdom because they will not study the Word. Instead, they take another man's perspective of the Word of God, and accept it as truth if it makes sense to them. They are avid conspiracy theorists, often spewing every doctrine, headline and theory to anyone who will hear them. They refuse to dedicate their bodies to holiness, and when confronted about their wicked ways, they sing the sinner's national anthem, "God knows my heart." After years of aimlessly waiting on God for a spouse, they give up on God, and go find their own spouses. They often end up back in fornication because their minds have not yet been renewed. Some even find themselves at the altar or the courthouse exchanging marital vows with another lost, but religious soul. They think their sins have produced good fruit for them, so they continue to spread their contaminated doctrines to anyone who will listen. Before long, their marriages begin to fail, and they find themselves getting further and further away from God when they feel their pleas and demands that He change their spouses are not being honored. Some even enter blatant witchcraft, while others find themselves abandoning their beliefs and following other religions. This is the life of a soul tied saint. They are slaves of sin, and many are still slaves to fornication. Yes, even those who practice abstinence! That's because their abstinence isn't practiced because they love and fear the Lord. Their abstinence is on a retractable leash. It'll only go as far as their demands. Their decisions to remain sexless is nothing but their attempts to make a deal with God, but make no mistake about it, they are still fornicators; they've simply become celibate fornicators. In their hearts they say to God, "If I remain abstinent, you must give me a husband." God won't make deals with the devil, and even though some saints are truly saved, they allow the devil to be their advisers, telling them how they ought to speak to God. God requires that we be righteous because we love Him, and not because we want something from Him. They seek God's hands, but not His heart. After years of abstinence, they feel God hasn't held up His end of the bargain, but of course, God never entered this wicked agreement with them. That's when they turn to their own devices and begin to search for their own husbands. They will tell anyone who'll listen to them that they waited for three, five, seven and ten years for their God-appointed husbands to show up. Secretly, they are angry with God for not serving their flesh, nevertheless, they know His name is honored, so they find crafty ways to call Him unfair. They say things like, "Girl, I waited seven and a half years for some man to come and tell me I was his wife. It never happened. I was abstinent the whole time. I got tired of waiting, so I decided to make things happen on my own, and that's when I met Jeff. Jeff isn't where he should be, but I know that he loves me." What she doesn't tell you is that:

- She regrets marrying Jeff.
- She's miserable with Jeff.
- Jeff cheats on her.
- Jeff hits on her.
- She sinned to get Jeff.
- She's never truly had a heart for God.
- She's always had a heart for herself.

- She's angry with God because He would not serve her.
- If she had to do it all again, she would not marry Jeff.

Instead, she will lead you to believe that she is happily married and her sin has produced many blessings for her. If you eat the lies she's serving, she will entice you into following the same path she's taken. Once you're married to an Ishmael who repeatedly disrespects and hurts you, she will finally open up to you about the hardships in her marriage to Jeff because you can now relate to her. She wasn't concerned about your happiness; she wanted someone to join her in her misery, and you looked desperate enough to follow her.

There are many soul tied saints in the church today who have not yet realized that they are the church. The key to being free is confessing your sins and asking God to free you from every illegal soul tie you've ever entered. Additionally, to stay free, you have to love God, and this won't happen if you don't know Him.

In other words, you have to read, study, and meditate on the Word of God until you have the attitude of God. You don't have to continue to live in bondage. Jesus is the key to your freedom.

What are Soul Ties?

The soul tie debate has been going on for thousands of years, but it is not only silly, it's unnecessary. The Bible doesn't specifically use the term "soul ties", but it does reference soul ties many times. The problem with today's church is that many of today's believers are legalistic and want everything printed word for word before they're willing to believe anything. Such thinking has led many believers further into bondage and opened them up to false doctrines, false prophets, false apostles and false leaders.

So, what are soul ties and can it be proven that they are real? Yes, soul ties are real and the truth is spelled out for us in the Bible.
Genesis 2:24: Therefore shall a man leave his father and his mother, and shall cleave unto his wife: and they shall be one flesh.

Webster's Revised Unabridged Dictionary

defines the word "cleave" as meaning:

1. *To adhere closely; to stick; to hold fast; to cling.*
2. *To unite or be united closely in interest or affection; to adhere with strong attachment.*
3. *To fit; to be adapted; to assimilate.*

When God said a man and his wife were to cleave together, He was saying the two should join themselves together just as their souls are joined. Of course, in many households, the spouses are joined together through soul ties, but they are divided by strife. Soul ties are established in the heart of a man (or woman), and therefore, anytime a soul tie is established, a heart is set up to be broken if the couple physically parts while still joined in the soulish realm.

The word "cleave" also has a second definition (in the English language), which means "to split". Nevertheless, God's definition of cleave means "to join". To get a better understanding of the word "cleave", let's reference the word "cleavage". The word "cleavage" means the area just above a woman's breast, especially if that area is exposed. It also references the split between the breasts of a woman. You'll notice that with younger women, the split is often wide because the breasts of a young woman tend to be perkier than the breasts of older women. Once a woman has a child or whenever she grows older, the space between her breasts will oftentimes appear almost non-existent because her breasts will begin to hang lower, causing them to appear closer together. Of course, perkier, younger breasts are more attractive to modern day society, but they are, in most cases, virgin breasts. This means they've never been used for breastfeeding or they're fairly new to the woman carrying them. Just like the woman herself, as breasts age, they lose their youthful appeal because they're backed by experience. As time passes, both breasts begin to cleave together as the space between them is filled in by experience. This is very similar to the way marriage works. When a couple first marries, they are often divided by inexperience and unfamiliarity, but as the couple ages, the gap between them grows smaller as they grow closer to one another. Not only do they have soul ties, but they learn to actually cleave to one another. Most divorces are the results of two people not cleaving to one another or one or both people being joined to other people.

David and Jonathan were the very first people to have their names linked as having been soul tied together. Of course, the two were men and had never had sex, therefore, their bond was one that was established because of their Philia love for one another. The word "Philia" means brotherly love.

1 Samuel 18:1 (KJV): And it came to pass, when he had made an end of speaking unto Saul, that the soul of Jonathan was knit with the soul of David, and Jonathan loved him as his own soul.

You'll notice that the Bible says Jonathan loved David as he loved his own soul, but it did not say that David loved Jonathan in the same manner. Now, if you've read the account of

David, Saul and Jonathan, you would clearly see that David loved Jonathan, but the author thought it important to mention that Jonathan's soul knit with David's soul. He didn't say that David's soul knit with Jonathan's. This is a very important piece of information because it not only tells us, in no uncertain terms, that soul ties are real, but it also helps us to understand that we can sometimes knit our souls to someone who has not knit their souls to us. In such cases, we will find ourselves loving that individual as we love ourselves, but we will not receive the same love in return. Of course, such soul ties are non-sexual, but anytime a couple has sex, they form soul ties with one another, even though they may or may not cleave to one another.

In 1 Samuel 18:1, we learn that Jonathan's soul knit to David's soul. Of course, the word "knit" means to tie together or join. Merriam Webster's Dictionary defines the word "knit" as:
1. *To closely join or combine (things or people).*
2. *To form (something) by bringing people*

or things together.

Biblically speaking, the word "knit" means to join as one or to cleave. We are one flesh with our spouses, or whomever we knit ourselves to, but we are one spirit with God. The same goes for believers. Many people are saved, but they don't have the heart of God. This means that they have not cleaved to the Word of God, but are instead, what the Bible refers to as "double-minded" and "unstable in all their ways".

Again, we see the word "soul" mentioned in 1 Samuel 18:1 and we see the word "knit". This means that two souls can knit together as one, and soul ties aren't always sexual. Some soul ties are established through friendship connections, and of course, we will almost always have soul ties with our closest of kin.

The soul is the meeting point between the flesh of a man and the spirit of a man, just as Jesus Christ is the meeting point between mankind and God. Jesus is the bridge that allows believers to access God through His own righteousness and shed blood. The soul is the bridge that allows information to cross over from the mind of a man into the spirit of a man. Unlike Christ Jesus, the soul does not filter lies from the truth. Instead, the spirit man will either accept or reject information because the spirit of a man belongs to God. The spirit of a man longs for God and is always in agreement with Him, but the soul of a man is mostly influenced by the strongest part of that man. If his flesh is stronger than his spirit (because of lack of knowledge), his soul will be misled by his flesh. If his spirit man is stronger than his flesh (because he's filled with the Word of God), his soul will be led by his spirit, and of course, the spirit of a believer is led by the Holy Spirit of God.

Whenever a soul is tied to another human being, that soul is simply linked or united to the soul of the other person. A soul tie can be Godly when it's established through Godly marriage or Godly associations, and a soul tie can be ungodly when it's established through fornication or ungodly associations. An ungodly soul tie will always lead to a broken heart. This doesn't necessarily mean the couple will break up, but it does mean they will hurt one another time and time again. That's because ungodly soul ties are often created by ungodly people or Godly people doing ungodly things.

God created soul ties to unite couples and to unite His people as one. However, Satan perverted this order by corrupting the people of God. A soul tie is the knitting of two souls as one, but of course, each person still bears their own mind, will and emotions. Nevertheless, make no mistake about it, soul ties do affect us in every way. Soul ties change the way we think, reason and the choices we make. Souls that are tied together are interwoven either through Godly marriage, Godly association or ungodly marriage and/ or association. Yes, soul ties are real and the truth is... a lot of people are still bound by them... even in the church!

Soul Ties Explained

Matthew 19:4-6 (NIV): "Haven't you read," he replied, "that at the beginning the Creator 'made them male and female,' and said, 'For this reason a man will leave his father and mother and be united to his wife, and the two will become one flesh'? So they are no longer two, but one flesh. Therefore what God has joined together, let no one separate."

In the 19th book of Matthew, we see the author referencing the bond of marriage. Of course, Jesus is the one speaking and He was answering a question posed to Him by the Pharisees. They'd asked Him if it was lawful for a man to divorce his wife and He explained to them that divorce was never an act permitted by God. The church in those days and the modern day church did not and still does not understand the biblical concept of marriage. Instead, many believers today enter marriage thinking it is a non-binding contractual agreement that states, in no uncertain terms, that they can try on their spouses for a few years, and if they believe their spouses aren't a good fit for their lives, they can divorce them. This means that the church has taken on the world's mindset in relation to marriage, and unlike God, the church does not hate divorces. Instead, many churches encourage divorce, especially if a believer has disobeyed God and married an unbeliever.

There are consequences to everything we do. Everything God created operates in seed time and harvest. We sow, and then, we reap. We sow again, and then, we reap again. If we don't like what's growing up for us, we've got to change our seeds or change the ground we're sowing in. We can't keep planting the same seeds and expecting a different harvest. Nevertheless, this is the reoccurring offense many believers find themselves practicing against the Lord God. Many believers disobey the Word and marry unbelievers, and then, when those unbelievers start behaving like unbelievers, they run to their pastors for help.

When their pastors can do nothing more than encourage them in the Lord, many believers turn to other ungodly behaviors such as emotionally or verbally abusing their spouses, physically attacking their spouses, and eventually divorcing their spouses. The truth is... we often marry two people when we go to the altar with unbelievers. We marry the person we imagine our soon-to-be spouses have the potential of becoming and we marry who they realistically are. We then attempt to remove the reality of who our spouses are, and we encourage them to become the people we've imagined they were deep down inside or have the potential to become. It's not long before we learn that a person who has not changed for God, will not change for us. This means that when we engage in ungodly practices, there are consequences for our actions, and sometimes, those consequences are painful to endure. This pain isn't designed to kill us; it comes to correct us, but the average believer tries to pray, chant, or tithe the pain away. When none of these things work, many begin to accuse God of being unfair, instead of simply acknowledging that they made a mistake and are now paying for that mistake. Believers don't need divorces; they need to repent.

I was 24 years old when I got married the first time. I was a babe in Christ, and as such, I was still very much in the world. It goes without saying that I went into sin and came out with a sinner. Did I know better? Yes. I knew that fornication was a sin. I knew that the man I was marrying was not a believer. I knew that I would be unequally yoked to him, but I married him anyway because I saw many of the qualities I wanted in a husband; plus, I liked his face. I thought I could change him. Like most women, I located what I believed to be the source of his misdirection, so I thought I could turn him around. I'd convinced myself that he'd never experienced true love, and I told myself that I would be a loving, faithful and supportive wife. In my mind, my "goodness" would rub off on him, and we'd live happily ever after. Well, the truth came in like a hurricane, and after seven years of marriage, we finally divorced. By this time, I'd grown up quite a bit in the Lord, and I'd spent most of my days talking about God, church and change. The start and ultimate failure of that marriage was my own fault, and I had to deal with the consequences of my actions, but did I learn the lesson I should have learned? No.

I got married again almost immediately after my first divorce was finalized. I met my second husband while going through a divorce with the first one. I'd matured somewhat in the Lord, but not enough to keep me away from sin. To stay away from sin, your love for the Lord has to grow up. I was still convinced that I could find my way around the Word to get what I wanted a lot faster. Again, I did whatever I thought was necessary to become his wife, including fornication.

While married the second time, the Lord began to grow me up at the rate of a heartbeat. I studied the Word more, and the more I studied the Word, the more I hungered for the Word. It was within that first year of marriage that the split in the marriage had become too evident to ignore. For the first time in my life, I'd truly repented of my fornication and my past sins. I repented and recommitted myself to God, but I still had to live with the consequences of my actions. You see, the problem with many believers is they think that after they repent, the problem should immediately disappear, but that's not how repentance works. To repent means to acknowledge your wrongs and turn your heart back to God, meaning, if you had the opportunity to engage in the very sin you were repenting for, you would not engage in it. Repenting doesn't remove whatever our sins have brought forward in our lives; for example, if a pregnant woman repents, her baby will not dissipate. She'll still be pregnant, and she will still give birth to her child. If a diseased man repents of the sin that brought that disease upon him, he will not be made whole again. Instead, he would remain diseased, unless, of course, he has the faith to be free and he applies that faith to his life. If a child repents at the end of the school year for not putting forth any effort into getting a passing grade, that child would still be retained. The point is... the consequences don't go away just because we've repented for our actions. I suffered through six years of marriage to my second husband, and it didn't matter how many times I attempted to repent, I kept waking up next to him. The point is... we go through the consequences so we can come to the conclusion that the Word of God is true and there's no way around it. Why didn't those marriages work?

1. I was already illegally married (soul tied) to other men. I hadn't truly repented for fornication, and that's why I fornicated with both of the men I'd married. Because there were other soul ties present in me, I could not fully give myself in marriage to any man.

2. My husbands were illegally married (soul tied) to other women. They were still unbelievers, so their sins were still very much present.

3. The foundation of our marriages was sin. I didn't marry because I wanted to serve God through marriage. I got married because I wanted to be loved by

someone, and given the "wife" title. To me, to be a wife, was one of the highest honors one could obtain.

4. I was unequally yoked in both marriages. Sure, we'd found a lot of sin in common, but spiritually speaking, I was further off than both men.

5. My mind hadn't been renewed. Without a renewed mind, it is hard for a marriage to work.

As I began to mature in the Lord, I had to accept the truth about myself, and I had to let the Word of God change me. I learned (in pain) and through my experiences that the Word of God will never return to Him void... ever. That's why it's never a good idea to encourage believers to take the easy way out. They need to truly repent, and until they do, they will continue to repeat the same behaviors that led them into their ungodly unions.

The Bible only recognizes the unmarried (virgins), married (non-virgins), and the widowed in relation to women. You can flip through any version of the bible available, and you will never see the term "girlfriend". Of course, any woman who was engaged to be married was, in most cases, betrothed to her husband-to-be, and already considered to be his wife, or better yet, *his* virgin. The marital agreement was established through a legal contract called the "kettubah." The couple were then "considered" to be married, even though the marital contract hadn't yet been fulfilled. That's because, biblically speaking, there is no such thing as an unwed non-virgin, unless, of course, the woman is a widow. Of course, as born again Christians, we can repent and ask the Lord to divorce us from our past lovers; that is, if we truly repent. Many people apologize, not understanding that apologizing to God is not the same as repenting. To apologize simply means to verbally say that you are sorry. To repent means to show that you are sorry by turning away from the sin you were in. Apologies come from the mouth, but repentance comes from the heart.

Many modern day churches do not know the

true definition of marriage, but have instead, accepted the world's definition of marriage. The world defines marriage as two people who are lawfully and legally joined together. Both parties have fulfilled their state's requirements to enter a lawful contract with one another, which states that the two will live together as husband and wife. Now, it goes without saying that the state's contractual agreement isn't binding, whereas, a couple can easily file for divorce or annulment for any reason whatsoever. The most common reason for divorce today is logged as "irreconcilable differences". Lawyers.com explains "irreconcilable differences" this way:

> *In most states, a spouse may get a no-fault divorce based on a breakdown of the marriage. Some states refer to this breakdown of a marriage as "irreconcilable differences." It means you and your spouse can't agree on basic, fundamental issues involving the marriage or your family, and you never will agree.*

Of course, the principle of irreconcilable differences goes against the very purpose of marriage and it goes against the Word of God. After all, marriage is a union that was established by God to be practiced by believers, but is now a part of the world's legal makeup. This means we cannot simply redefine marriage, but we have to honor God's original design for marriage.

Since the world has taken the Christian concept of marriage and attempted to redefine it, divorce rates are at their highest... even in the church. That's because many believers have not yet separated themselves from the world. Many believers have attempted to build or cross bridges between the secular world and the church, and this bridge simply does not exist, nor will it ever exist. As a result, many believers are now neck-deep or drowning in their lukewarm rivers of religiousness.

So, what exactly is marriage then? Marriage does not occur when two people stand at the altar and exchange vows! Marriage occurs the very moment two or more people sexually engage with one another! That's why God said the two shall be one! As we continue in this chapter, I'm going to list a few biblical examples of marriages established through sexual contact, both legal and illegal. First, we need to discuss the history of marriage.

In the Old Testament days, marriages between Jews were arranged and most men married the women their parents had chosen for them. In some cases, the bride had been chosen for the groom while they were still infants, toddlers or children. In other instances, the bride had been chosen or picked once the son became an adult or reached a certain age. In other words, some brides were called, while others were chosen. A called bride would be a woman who'd been betrothed to a man since her childhood. She had already been set aside to be that man's wife, therefore, it could be assumed that she was likely taught to serve as that particular man's wife from the moment she was betrothed. A woman who was chosen, on the other hand, didn't have the luxury (or agony) of knowing who her groom would be or if she'd ever get married. Nevertheless, she was taught to perform the household duties of a wife, and she was taught the roles, responsibilities and expectations that she would one day have as a wife. She was not taught to be the wife of the man who'd chosen her because he'd come later in her life, and therefore, she had to learn her husband's wants and needs after they were married.

It goes without saying that in those times, many of the men were not happy with the wives their parents' had chosen for them. Because of this, they would devise ways to divorce their wives, and the only way out of marriage (at that time) was adultery. The wife would've had to commit adultery while married to her husband, which, of course, came with a death sentence, or the husband would have to prove that his wife had played the harlot before they'd gotten married. This means the wife was not a virgin when he'd married her, and the only excusable time for a woman who was not a virgin to marry was if she was a widow. A married woman was and still is any woman who's engaged in sexual activity with a man.

The husbands who did not like their parents' pick would sometimes lie on their wives by saying they'd discovered that their wives had slept with someone else before marrying them. If their claims could be proven, their marriages would be considered null and void, since Jewish law did not permit two men to marry one woman. The woman would then be judged as an adulteress and stoned to death. Of course, this practice was barbaric and cruel, but it was Jewish law.

To prove their daughters' innocence, the fathers of the brides would always keep the proof of their daughters' pre-wedding purity. This proof would be in the form of a white cloth. When the couple married, the father of the bride would present the groom with a white cloth. The couple would consummate the marriage on this white cloth, and in many cases, when the hymen had been broken, blood would be shed. This blood served as evidence that the maiden had been a virgin before her groom "deflowered" her. The "deflowering" of the bride took place at the parents of the bride's home while witnesses waited outside the bedroom. The cloth would then be given back to the eagerly awaiting father-in-law and he would put it away for safe keeping. If the groom decided that he wanted to divorce his wife by claiming she'd played the harlot, the father-in-law and the witnesses would come before the elders alongside the groom. The father-in-law would present the tokens (white cloth) of his daughter's purity, and the husband would be made to pay one hundred shekels to the girl's father. The point is... in those days, they understood that marriage was established through sex and not wedding vows. The only vows said in biblical marriages were the agreements or bonds agreed upon by both father-in-laws or the father-in-law and the groom. Nevertheless, couples did not have the traditional weddings we have today. Instead, on the agreed upon date of their daughters' release, most parents would host a wedding reception to celebrate the marriage that was about to occur between their daughter and her soon-to-be groom. Once the party was over, the groom would take his bride to a room prepared for them in her parents' house, and he'd join himself to her through sex. After sex happened, she was no longer considered a single woman. She was a wife, and as such, she could no longer wear the garments of a virgin.

Deuteronomy 22:13-21 (NIV): If a man takes a wife and, after sleeping with her, dislikes her and slanders her and gives her a bad name, saying, "I married this woman, but when I approached her, I did not find proof of her virginity," then the young woman's father and mother shall bring to the town elders at the gate proof that she was a virgin. Her father will say to the elders, "I gave my daughter in marriage to this man, but he dislikes her. Now he has slandered her and said, 'I did not find your daughter to be a virgin.' But here is the proof of my daughter's virginity." Then her parents shall display the cloth before the elders of the town, and the elders shall take the man and punish him. They shall fine him a hundred shekels of silver and give them to the young woman's father, because this man has given an Israelite virgin a bad name. She shall continue to be his wife; he must not divorce her as long as he lives. If, however, the charge is true and no proof of the young woman's virginity can be found, she shall be brought to the door of her father's house and there the men of her town shall stone her to death. She has done an outrageous thing in Israel by being promiscuous while still in her father's house. You must purge the evil from among you.

There's a troubling story in the Bible that best illustrates how marriages were viewed. The story is that of Amnon and his sister Tamar. **2 Samuel 13:1-19 (NIV):** In the course of time, Amnon son of David fell in love with Tamar, the beautiful sister of Absalom son of David. Amnon became so obsessed with his sister Tamar that he made himself ill. She was a virgin, and it seemed impossible for him to do anything to her.
Now Amnon had an adviser named Jonadab

son of Shimeah, David's brother. Jonadab was a very shrewd man. He asked Amnon, "Why do you, the king's son, look so haggard morning after morning? Won't you tell me?"

Amnon said to him, "I'm in love with Tamar, my brother Absalom's sister."

"Go to bed and pretend to be ill," Jonadab said. "When your father comes to see you, say to him, 'I would like my sister Tamar to come and give me something to eat. Let her prepare the food in my sight so I may watch her and then eat it from her hand.'"

So Amnon lay down and pretended to be ill. When the king came to see him, Amnon said to him, "I would like my sister Tamar to come and make some special bread in my sight, so I may eat from her hand."

David sent word to Tamar at the palace: "Go to the house of your brother Amnon and prepare some food for him." So Tamar went to the house of her brother Amnon, who was lying down. She took some dough, kneaded it, made the bread in his sight and baked it. Then she took the pan and served him the bread, but he refused to eat.

"Send everyone out of here," Amnon said. So everyone left him. Then Amnon said to Tamar, "Bring the food here into my bedroom so I may eat from your hand." And Tamar took the bread she had prepared and brought it to her brother Amnon in his bedroom. But when she took it to him to eat, he grabbed her and said, "Come to bed with me, my sister." "No, my brother!" she said to him. "Don't force me! Such a thing should not be done in Israel! Don't do this wicked thing. What about me? Where could I get rid of my disgrace? And what about you? You would be like one of the wicked fools in Israel. Please speak to the king; he will not keep me from being married to you." But he refused to listen to her, and since he was stronger than she, he raped her.

Then Amnon hated her with intense hatred. In fact, he hated her more than he had loved her. Amnon said to her, "Get up and get out!" "No!" she said to him. "Sending me away would be a greater wrong than what you have already done to me."

But he refused to listen to her. He called his personal servant and said, "Get this woman out of my sight and bolt the door after her." So his servant put her out and bolted the door after her. She was wearing an ornate robe, for this was the kind of garment the virgin daughters of the king wore. Tamar put ashes on her head and tore the ornate robe she was wearing. She put her hands on her head and went away, weeping aloud as she went.

What happened in this story? Amnon was lustfully attracted to his sister. Of course, in those times, incestuous relationships were not considered taboo, especially when the siblings had different mothers. Amnon could have easily asked his father, David, for Tamar's hand in marriage, but like many men, he wanted the perks of marriage without the responsibility of a wife. He was a wicked man who'd selfishly taken advantage of his own sister.

Tamar begged Amnon to simply ask their father for her hand in marriage. She even tried to reason with him, reminding him of the shame she would suffer and the label he would wear, but he didn't care. He raped her, and then, after he raped her, he discovered something very important. He discovered that the love he once had for her wasn't real love; it was lust. He then hated his sister and tried to send her away, but Tamar didn't want to go away from her rapist at this point. She said to him that sending her away was even more wicked than the rape itself. Why was this? Even after raping her, Amnon had the chance to honor Tamar by asking their father for her hand in marriage, because they were now in fornication. Contrary to popular belief (and doctrines), fornication is not premarital sex. There is no such thing as premarital sex, since a couple becomes married in the eyes of God the moment they have sex with one another. Fornication is illegal sex, and one form of fornication (in the biblical days) was having sex with a woman without asking her father for his permission. It meant to join one's self to a woman without honoring the Old Testament law in regards to marital order. This means the man did not:

1. Ask for the woman's hand in marriage.
2. Make a vow to the father to honor,

protect and love his daughter for the rest of his life.
3. Pay the dowry price for the bride.
4. Deflower the maiden on the white cloth provided by her father. Again, this was designed to protect her honor and the family's name.

Instead, he deceptively and wickedly joined himself to a woman, making it illegal for any other man to legally have her. He would then return her to her father's house, forcing her father to provide for her for the rest of his life, or if the sex had been consensual, the woman could be stoned to death. In other words, the man robbed the father-in-law of his bride price, he robbed the family of their honor, and more importantly, he robbed the woman of any chance to ever be (legally) married to a man or to have children. Instead, she would be a public shame and would likely spend her days being judged, ridiculed and maybe even physically attacked. Fornication didn't just affect the woman involved; it affected the entire family as a whole.

Tamar didn't want Amnon to send her away from him, because this was the equivalent of a divorce and a guarantee that she would likely never (legally) marry, conceive children or be able to lift her head in public again. She was the king's daughter, so she would be a public spectacle for the people to laugh at and scorn. Even after being raped, she attempted to remain in her brother's room, hoping that he would honor her by asking their father for her hand in marriage. When he would not, she tore her virgin's garments and put ashes on her head. The ashes represented sorrow and grieving. She tore her garments because it was considered immoral (and probably illegal) for a woman who was not a virgin to wear a virgin's garments. Tamar was publicly acknowledging that she had been raped and was no longer available for marriage. If you go on to read the entire story, you will learn that Absalom saw his sister and asked her if Amnon had slept with her. When she acknowledged that she had been raped, Absalom began to hate his brother, and two years later, he lured him to his death. The Bible tells us that Absalom killed

Amnon, because he raped his sister, but I suspect that it goes much deeper than that. I believe that Absalom killed Amnon, because not only did he rape his sister, but he had two years to right his wrong. He could have removed the dishonor from Tamar, but he didn't. Instead, he allowed her to live as a disgraced woman, and at the same time, Tamar could never remarry as long as Amnon was alive. Killing Amnon removed the dishonor from Tamar and made her available to remarry, nevertheless, she would be considered a widow.

Deuteronomy 22:28-29 (NIV): If a man happens to meet a virgin who is not pledged to be married and rapes her and they are discovered, he shall pay her father fifty shekels of silver. He must marry the young woman, for he has violated her. He can never divorce her as long as he lives.

To "marry the young woman" means he must follow the proper protocol to acknowledge her as his wife. The King James Version of the Bible says that the man has "humbled" the woman by raping her. The word "humble" is derived from the Latin word "humus" which means "ground" or "low". Of course, the word "humus" is where the words human, humble and humiliate originate. To be human means you are made from the dust of the ground. To be humble means to acknowledge, oftentimes through meekness and servitude, that you are made from the dust of the ground, and to be humiliated is to be publicly reminded that you are made from dirt. Google's Online Dictionary defines "humbled" as:

1. *Of low social, administrative, or political rank.*
2. *Lower (someone) in dignity or importance.*

Now, we can better understand how fornication affects women. It lowers our self-perception and self-esteem. Fornication humiliates us, and when a woman has been humiliated many times, she will oftentimes attempt to puff herself up in pride to enable herself to walk unashamedly in the midst of the people she believes will scorn or ridicule her. After all, being used is humiliating. Anytime a man lies with a woman, and then, walks away from her, he takes a part of her with him. Of course, God will restore her if she repents, but the truth is, there are many sectioned off men and women running to the altars to marry what's left of themselves to other people. When their spouses discover that there are important pieces of their lovers that are missing, it is common for those spouses to begin looking for those missing pieces. For example, a husband who's married to a distant wife will oftentimes search his wife's heart (through conversation) to find out where the rest of her heart is. He will intentionally engage her in conversations about her past lovers and her past as a whole, and he will pay attention to the people she speaks mostly of. He may also pay attention to her online searches, her associations and who they're connected to and her habits. This is his attempt to find his whole wife, and in most cases, he will be successful at finding the missing pieces of his wife's soul, but he may not be successful recovering those pieces.

Judges 19:1-30 (ESV): In those days, when there was no king in Israel, a certain Levite was sojourning in the remote parts of the hill country of Ephraim, who took to himself a concubine from Bethlehem in Judah. And his concubine was unfaithful to him, and she went away from him to her father's house at Bethlehem in Judah, and was there some four months. Then her husband arose and went after her, to speak kindly to her and bring her back. He had with him his servant and a couple of donkeys. And she brought him into her father's house. And when the girl's father saw him, he came with joy to meet him. And his father-in-law, the girl's father, made him stay, and he remained with him three days. So they ate and drank and spent the night there. And on the fourth day they arose early in the morning, and he prepared to go, but the girl's father said to his son-in-law, "Strengthen your heart with a morsel of bread, and after that you may go." So the two of them sat and ate and drank together. And the girl's father said to the man, "Be pleased to spend the night, and let your heart be merry." And when the man rose up to go, his father-in-law pressed him, till he spent the night there again. And on the fifth day he arose early in the morning to depart. And the girl's father said, "Strengthen your heart and wait until the day declines." So they ate, both of them. And when the man and his concubine and his servant rose up to depart, his father-in-law, the girl's father, said to him, "Behold, now the day has waned toward evening. Please, spend the night. Behold, the day draws to its close. Lodge here and let your heart be merry, and tomorrow you shall arise early in the morning for your journey, and go home."

But the man would not spend the night. He rose up and departed and arrived opposite Jebus (that is, Jerusalem). He had with him a couple of saddled donkeys, and his concubine was with him. When they were near Jebus, the day was nearly over, and the servant said to his master, "Come now, let us turn aside to this city of the Jebusites and spend the night in it." And his master said to him, "We will not turn aside into the city of foreigners, who do not belong to the people of Israel, but we will pass on to

Gibeah." And he said to his young man, "Come
and let us draw near to one of these places and
spend the night at Gibeah or at Ramah." So
they passed on and went their way. And the
sun went down on them near Gibeah, which
belongs to Benjamin, and they turned aside
there, to go in and spend the night at Gibeah.
And he went in and sat down in the open
square of the city, for no one took them into
his house to spend the night.
And behold, an old man was coming from his
work in the field at evening. The man was from
the hill country of Ephraim, and he was
sojourning in Gibeah. The men of the place
were Benjaminites. And he lifted up his eyes
and saw the traveler in the open square of the
city. And the old man said, "Where are you
going? And where do you come from?" And he
said to him, "We are passing from Bethlehem in
Judah to the remote parts of the hill country of
Ephraim, from which I come. I went to
Bethlehem in Judah, and I am going to the
house of the Lord, but no one has taken me
into his house. We have straw and feed for our
donkeys, with bread and wine for me and your

female servant and the young man with your servants. There is no lack of anything." And the old man said, "Peace be to you; I will care for all your wants. Only, do not spend the night in the square." So he brought him into his house and gave the donkeys feed. And they washed their feet, and ate and drank.

As they were making their hearts merry, behold, the men of the city, worthless fellows, surrounded the house, beating on the door. And they said to the old man, the master of the house, "Bring out the man who came into your house, that we may know him." And the man, the master of the house, went out to them and said to them, "No, my brothers, do not act so wickedly; since this man has come into my house, do not do this vile thing. Behold, here are my virgin daughter and his concubine. Let me bring them out now. Violate them and do with them what seems good to you, but against this man do not do this outrageous thing." But the men would not listen to him. So the man seized his concubine and made her go out to them. And they knew her and abused her all night until the morning. And as the dawn began to break, they let her go. And as morning appeared, the woman came and fell down at the door of the man's house where her master was, until it was light.

And her master rose up in the morning, and when he opened the doors of the house and went out to go on his way, behold, there was his concubine lying at the door of the house, with her hands on the threshold. He said to her, "Get up, let us be going." But there was no answer. Then he put her on the donkey, and the man rose up and went away to his home. And when he entered his house, he took a knife, and taking hold of his concubine he divided her, limb by limb, into twelve pieces, and sent her throughout all the territory of Israel. And all who saw it said, "Such a thing has never happened or been seen from the day that the people of Israel came up out of the land of Egypt until this day; consider it, take counsel, and speak."

This story has many, many lessons in it, but first, let's explore some of the terms. First off, we see the term "concubine". What exactly is a concubine? Google's Online Dictionary defines "concubine" as:

- *(in polygamous societies) a woman who lives with a man, but has lower status than his wife or wives.*

We could easily determine that the concubine is not regarded as a wife, but that's not entirely true. The concubine, in biblical days, was pretty much the lowest wife, meaning, she was a secondary wife. Here are a few differences:

1. The groom paid a dowry price for the wife, but he did not pay the concubine.
2. A concubine's main purpose was sex, but the men of that day understood that after joining themselves to her, they were responsible for providing her with a place to stay, food to eat, and whatever needs she had. In other words, she was treated somewhat similar to the "official" wife, meaning, the wife that was recognized by society.
3. The "official" wife wore special garments for her "wedding day" and she

oftentimes had bridesmaids. Again, there was no exchanging of vows between a man and his bride, but instead, moreso of an agreement between the parents of the bride and the groom or the groom and his father-in-law.

4. Wives often had receptions for their "official" marriages, but with concubines, there was no reception. The groom simply took her to be (in modern day terms) one of his whores. Nevertheless, the concubine was bound by the same laws as the "official" wife, so if she had committed adultery with another man, she would be stoned to death.

5. With wives, there was often a betrothal (reservation to marry), but a man finding and taking a concubine was oftentimes a random act.

6. The parents of concubines were oftentimes slaves.

7. Men often chose their own concubines, whereas, their parents chose their wives.

8. Concubines were oftentimes brought in

when a wife was barren. This was to ensure that the husband bore children for himself.

9. Women were uneducated in those days and relied solely on their male counterparts. For example, if a woman's father and brothers were dead, she would likely consider concubinage if she was not betrothed to marry and no other male in her family took her under his authority. Concubinage was a more acceptable status than prostitution.

10. Men of great wealth and esteem often had many concubines, and this, of course, was an act of greed on the man's part. Men, in those days, wanted as many children as possible, therefore, concubines allowed a man to "increase his legacy" on earth.

11. Like the "official" wife, a concubine was a virgin before being deflowered by her groom, nevertheless, it was not uncommon for a man to "give" his concubine to another man to sleep with. If someone else slept with a man's

concubine, that man would likely continue providing food, shelter and basic necessities for his concubine, but he would not sleep with her anymore. This is evidenced in the story of King David and his son, Absalom. Absalom wanted to take the kingdom from his father, so in a despicable act of treason, he pitched a tent on the roof of his father's castle. He did this act so that all Israel could know he had taken his father's concubines. After Absalom's death, David grieved for his son, and the Bible tells us in 2 Samuel 20 that David took the ten concubines he had left to watch the castle, put them in a house that was under guard (protected by security), and he continued to provide for them, but he never slept with them again. The Bible said they lived the rest of their lives like widows.

Let's go back to the story of the man and his concubine. You'll notice that in the story, the author refers to the concubine's father as her lover's father-in-law. Again, this is to denote that the two were officially married, just not legally married.

Now that we have a better understanding of who the concubine is, we need to have a clearer understanding of the line that says she was unfaithful to him. The term "unfaithful" wasn't used in this text to say that she had slept with another man. She was unfaithful to him because she'd left him and moved back in with her father. In those days, such an act was uncustomary and pretty much illegal because the wife and the concubine were seen as the property of their husbands. The concubine's family and the concubine herself were oftentimes slaves of the groom's family.

It is unclear why the concubine's father tried to keep her husband from leaving, and it could be said that the author himself is implying that the father of the concubine may have been conspiring against his son-in-law. Nevertheless, the matter was not further explored, so we are left to draw our own conclusions. We do see, however, that the husband of the concubine found himself in a dangerous situation. He was sojourning (sleeping over) to a stranger's house when the men of that city began to bang on the man's door, demanding that he send the traveler out so they could "know him". First off, it was not uncommon for a person to let a traveler into their home if they thought the traveler was a decent or well-esteemed man. Next off, you'll notice that the traveler's servant requested that they turn off to a city named Jebus, but the man did not want to go into Jebus because the Jebusites were pagans. They were not of the tribe of Israel, therefore, anyone who was not an Israelite was a pagan. The author is sure to mention that the traveler did the honorable thing by staying in a city inhabited by Israelites, and these Israelites were from the tribe of Benjamin. They were called Benjamites, and this particular branch of the tribe of Israel had turned away from the Lord and had been practicing homosexuality. Such a thing was not only detestable in Israel, but by law, the crime of homosexuality was punishable by death. The reason the author mentions that the traveler chose not to stay with pagans is because he wants to show that the man stayed amongst people he considered to be his brethren, people he trusted. These people were supposed to be following the Old Testament law, but instead, they had turned away from God. The word "know" in this text means the men were planning to rape the traveler who, of course, was a man himself.

Next, we see that the owner of the home tried to protect his guest by offering his own virgin daughter and the man's concubine for the men to "violate", or better yet, sleep with. This tells us that the owner's guest was a man he believed to be of great importance because a man's virgin daughter was a token of honor for the family. By offering her up, the host himself was offering the family's good name as a sacrifice to protect his guest. Why he offered the man's concubine is a mystery, but as the text goes on, we come to see that the traveler seized his own concubine and handed her to the men. Of course, he was trying to protect the family name of the man who had so kindly allowed him to lodge at his house.

The wicked men took the concubine, repeatedly raped and abused her, and then, they allowed her to go free. She returned to the house of the host, where she died on the threshold of the door. When her husband woke up the next day, he found her lifeless body. The question is: Why did he cut her body into twelve pieces? There's a lot of speculation in the Christian church about this strange act, nevertheless, some of his reasons are clear:

1. There were twelve tribes of Israel. He cut the woman's body up into twelve pieces and sent them throughout Israel into every tribe to sound the alarm.

2. We could see his last act against his concubine as an even more treacherous act than the rape itself, but the truth is, he was grieving. He wanted all of Israel to know what had happened to his concubine; he wanted to bring judgment upon Benjamin, and he wanted his concubine's rapists/ killers to pay for their crimes. Sending body parts

to each tribe would certainly get their attention and alert them to the urgency of the matter. This would ensure a swift judgment because this act got the people to talking. Truthfully, he could have buried her and went on with his life, but he didn't. He made sure that the men of Benjamin were punished for their crimes.

3. Every time a man lies down with a woman, he joins himself to her, and the two become one flesh in the eyes of the Lord. It can be said that dismembering her body not only served to get the people of Israel's attention, but it sent a clear message that she was no longer "one" with him. Her soul had been scattered by every man who'd lain with her.

Some people would even ask, "If he loved her, why would he send her out to be raped?" For us, this act is treacherous, wicked and uncalled for, but you have to understand that we are in a different time. Back then, a concubine was nothing but a sex slave. The man understood that the men who came out to rape him weren't going to leave. They were determined to quench their fiery lusts, and he didn't want the daughter of the host to be raped because she was a virgin. If her father gave her to the men of that city to rape, his family's name would have been ruined. However, if a man's concubine was raped, it did nothing to his own name; instead, he'd likely continue to provide for her, but he would never sleep with her again. You'll notice that after the concubine had been raped, her husband had initially thought she was alive. He told her to get up so they could leave, meaning, he was going to continue to his residence with her.

Soul ties are just as real today as they were in the biblical days. To be soul tied to someone, in the romantic sense, simply means to be legally or illegally married to that person. As the years went by, marriage was somehow redefined to mean a non-binding legal contract between a husband and his wife. I suspect this change happened when the church went under the law, whereas, it had initially been over the law. By the church, I mean the Catholic Church. The Catholic Church was the law at one point, but a wicked king (King Henry, VIII of England) desperate to divorce his wife, changed the arrangement, giving the law power (sovereign supremacy) over the church. Of course, God never changed His definition of marriage, and as such, many people are illegally married to this day! Again, we can repent and let God free us from every soul tie established through fornication, and after this process is complete, we are free to remarry, but only in the Lord.

Genesis 34:1-5: Now Dinah, the daughter Leah had borne to Jacob, went out to visit the women of the land. When Shechem son of Hamor the Hivite, the ruler of that area, saw her, he took her and raped her. His heart was drawn to Dinah daughter of Jacob; he loved the young woman and spoke tenderly to her. And Shechem said to his father Hamor, "Get me this girl as my wife."
When Jacob heard that his daughter Dinah had been defiled, his sons were in the fields with his

livestock; so he did nothing about it until they came home.

What exactly happened here? Shechem was obviously a proud and entitled man who thought he could have whatever and whomever he wanted. Of course, he was not a Jewish man, but was instead, a Canaanite. It was unlawful and despicable for a Jew to intermarry with a Caananite, but Jacob had moved his family to the city of Shechem, located in Canaan. When the ruler's son, Shechem, saw Dinah, he took it upon himself to take her as his wife. The Bible says that Dinah had been "defiled", but this isn't just a reference to the illegal sex that had taken place. This defilement occurred because she was joined to a Canaanite. Again, you'll notice that the problem here is that the father of the bride had not been consulted before sex had taken place. He was consulted (and humiliated) after the fact. Think of it this way. Imagine taking your four year old daughter to a beauty shop. You ask the beautician to simply braid her hair, but instead, the beautician takes it upon herself to cut your daughter's hair. To add insult to injury, she then attempts to charge you for the haircut you didn't ask for. For one, your daughter was too young for the haircut the beautician gave her, and more importantly, you didn't ask for the haircut. Instead of paying the beautician, you'd likely take her to court and seek damages. That's how Jacob felt. He took his daughter to a city, and he never gave Shechem permission to have her. Instead, Shechem took her for himself, raped her, and then, offered to pay for her hand in marriage. Such an act was not only dishonorable, but it was no different than calling the woman a prostitute. As a matter of fact, Dinah's brothers avenged her rape by killing the men of Shechem, and when their father (Jacob) confronted them about their actions, they made it very clear that they saw Shechem's act as degrading towards Dinah. "But they replied, "Should he have treated our sister like a prostitute?" (Genesis 34:31).

Sexual Vs. Emotional Soul Ties

If you're a guy, you've probably heard a few women say that if their spouses were to cheat on them, they would rather it be a sexual relationship versus an emotional one. If you're a woman, you've likely spoken those words or heard another woman speak them.

No (sane) woman wants her husband to cheat on her; that goes without saying. Nevertheless, if a man is going to cheat, the average woman would prefer it be a sexual relationship with no emotions involved as opposed to an emotional relationship where the two are sharing intimate details of their lives with one another. The reason for this is that most women understand that there are some guys out there who are sexually greedy. Of course, no woman wants to end up being the wife of such a soul, but having brothers, cousins and uncles, a lot of women have witnessed how far some men will go for sexual favors. We've also witnessed those same brothers, cousins and uncles speak reproachfully about the women they were sleeping with. They didn't love those women, and they had no plans for the future with them. Their relationships were entirely centered around sex and nothing else. For this reason, most married women (if they had to choose) would prefer to have a man who opens his pants to another woman than a man who opens his heart to another woman. Most women would prefer a man who's sexually soul tied to another woman than a man who's emotionally soul tied to another woman.

What's the difference between sexual soul ties and emotional soul ties? Of course, sexual soul ties are established through sexual intercourse and they join the people in body and soul, but emotional soul ties are established through emotional intimacy, and they join the hearts of the people involved. Of course, sexual soul ties affect our emotions, but emotional soul ties have the power to change our minds and our plans. For example, a married man who's sexually soul tied to his mistress can easily walk away from her, as opposed to a married man who has opened his heart to his mistress.

Sexual Soul Ties

God designed sex, so it isn't a bad thing when used in the way God designed it. Of course, Satan went behind God and perverted just about everything God designed. The enemy wants mankind to enjoy the benefits of sex without accepting the responsibilities that come with sex. For example, a man should only have sex with a woman after they've exchanged vows in the presence of two or three witnesses, and of course, with a man or woman of faith present. Additionally, they are to honor the marital laws of the country, city or state they are living in. After sex occurs, the man is supposed to provide for, pray for, cover, protect and lead the wife he's just taken onto himself. He is also supposed to raise, protect, provide for, correct, lead and nurture the children who are birthed in his marital union. These are his God-given responsibilities. Satan pretty much tosses out the responsibilities and encourages men to uncover women without covering them, meaning, to take off their clothes and have sex with them, without fulfilling the God-instituted roles of being husbands. When a man has sex with a woman outside of the manner in which God designed, he will establish an ungodly soul tie with that woman. This means that God is not the third-fold in their union; Satan is.

God designed marriage to last a lifetime, but Satan perverted marriage to fail. Satan understands the makeup of human beings, so he understands that the body was not designed for fornication. He understands that fornication will ultimately destroy the body or ruin the life of the person participating in it. He also understands that divorce rips a hole in the soul of almost everyone who's ever been through it. Ask any divorced person and they will tell you that divorce feels a whole lot like death. It's not only a painful event, but it's demeaning, humiliating and confusing. Nevertheless, Satan perverted marriage by encouraging the people in it to sex their way into an ungodly union with one another, and then, attempt to make it right by exchanging vows after they've cut God out of the picture. Most people who do this don't truly understand soul ties, the purpose of Godly marriage and how fornication affects one's marriage. Because of this, most people who get married do so while being illegally and unknowingly married to other people. This makes each individual almost impossible to deal with, because when you enter a Godly union bound by an ungodly soul tie, you won't be able to truly cleave to your spouse. Instead, the two of you will try to manipulate one another to force a fit, but it won't happen. It's similar to taking a puzzle piece and trying to force or alter it to fit into the puzzle you've put together. If the piece doesn't fit, you simply need to find the right piece. When two souls are joining as one, they need to be transformed by the renewing of their minds so that they can fit together without the bumps and the lumps created by ungodly soul ties.

Most believers understand sexual soul ties to an extent, but they don't understand how sexual soul ties behave. Because of this, many in the church today find themselves going from one relationship to the next, trying to figure out why they can't seem to find their soulmates. They don't realize that their souls are already tied to other human beings, and the people they are trying to romantically link themselves to are also bound. God said His people perish from lack of knowledge. There are so many people praying deep, lengthy and passionate prayers for spouses, and these people can't seem to get their prayers through to God because they have rejected knowledge! **Hosea 4:6 (ESV):** My people are destroyed for lack of knowledge; because you have rejected knowledge, I reject you from being a priest to me. And since you have forgotten the law of your God, I also will forget your children.

God hears the prayers of His people, but since He has already said "yes" to the desires of our hearts, He doesn't answer our prayers by giving us the things we want. He answers our prayers by showing us what's keeping us from receiving the "yes" and the "amen" He has already spoken. In other words, He shows us a reflection of ourselves, and all too often, we reject the knowledge God is handing us, and continue to pray religious prayers that rise up to fall down. The truth is... we don't need new relationships or more money... we need knowledge, deliverance and renewed minds! **James 4:3 (NIV):** When you ask, you do not receive, because you ask with wrong motives, that you may spend what you get on your pleasures.

Illegal sexual soul ties bring friction between the people involved. That's because it is next to impossible for a woman to separate sex from her emotions because women were not made that way. When you come across a woman who is able to separate sex from her feelings, please know that she is a severely broken soul, and as such, she's become numb to the effects of ungodly soul ties. This means she's likely married to several men through sex, and she's used to being an object to men. Men, on the other hand, aren't emotional creatures, and because of this, men can easily separate sex from emotions. Nevertheless, contrary to popular belief, this does not mean that meaningful or meaningless sex does not affect men. Sex affects men the most because God holds a man responsible morally, spiritually and financially for every woman he lies with! At the same time, the more a man engages in illegal sex, the harder his heart becomes. That's because he begins to pick up one of the traits that serial killers have, and that's the ability to see people as objects instead of humans. In other words, he slowly loses his ability to empathize! You'll notice that the most promiscuous of men tend to have problems with their finances, in their "serious" relationships, on their jobs, and in their lives. A woman's scars are oftentimes open and on display for the world to see, but the scars left on a man's soul are oftentimes hidden in plain sight. Ungodly sexual soul ties lead to unmet expectations, and these unmet expectations lead to friction, hurt and betrayal.

Emotional Soul Ties

Emotional soul ties can be dangerous because they often involve two or more people who have opened their hearts to one another. Emotional soul ties are good when God has made the connections, but they are dangerous and ungodly when they are established by human beings. Why is this? Soul ties were not created to be managed by human beings. Soul ties were created to be managed by God. God has to be the third fold in the cord between human beings, otherwise, spouses will not operate as units, but will instead, operate as individuals. You'll notice that the root word of "individual" is "divide". God does not want married couples to operate as individuals because this would destroy their marriages. A couple must operate as a unit for marriage to work. He created couples to operate as one body, and anytime a member of the body does not cooperate, it is considered "dead", and therefore, will be amputated.

Matthew 12:25 (ESV): Knowing their thoughts, he said to them, "Every kingdom divided against itself is laid waste, and no city or house divided against itself will stand.

Mark 10:6-9 (ESV): But from the beginning of creation, 'God made them male and female.'

'Therefore a man shall leave his father and mother and hold fast to his wife, and the two shall become one flesh.' So they are no longer two but one flesh. What therefore God has joined together, let not man separate.

Emotional soul ties are oftentimes established through our day-to-day contact, and these soul ties are easily established, but difficult to break free of. That's because, unlike sexual soul ties, emotional soul ties involve every aspect of our souls: mind, will and emotions. People can oftentimes separate their feelings from sex, especially if their souls are already preoccupied with other ungodly soul ties, but emotional soul ties occur when people will themselves to open up to one another.

There are different types of emotional soul ties, and they include familiar soul ties, romantic soul ties and friendly soul ties.
Familiar Soul Ties- These soul ties are the soul ties we have with our family members. Even though these bonds can be very tight, they aren't as important as the soul tie between a

man and his wife. Familiar soul ties can be Godly or ungodly. An example of a Godly, familiar soul tie is that of a mother who encourages her children in the Lord. She allows her children to make their own choices and mistakes, and she prays for her children without fail. An example of an ungodly familiar soul tie is that of a mother who controls her adult children. Instead of allowing her children to make their own choices and mistakes, she berates them and preys on them for her own selfish gain, gratification or reputation. She is controlling, manipulative and self-righteous.

Friendly Soul Ties- Friendly soul ties are the bonds we willfully establish with the people we refer to as our friends, co-workers and distant family members. These soul ties are oftentimes the strongest of all soul ties, depending, of course, on our beliefs, cultures and experiences. In friendly soul ties, we often share the most intimate of our secrets, and we also tend to bestow the greatest amount of trust upon the people we refer to as our friends.

Romantic Soul Ties- The only time a romantic soul tie is considered Godly is when it is the joining force between a man and his wife. A married couple's soul tie is more emotional than it is sexual. If one of the spouses was to emotionally neglect the other spouse, their sexual relationship will be directly impacted since emotional, soul ties will either strengthen or weaken a couple's sexual relationship and vice versa.

In familiar soul ties, we don't always have the luxury of hiding our secrets. Instead, our family members have watched us grow and have seen many of the mistakes we've made along the way. In friendly soul ties, we choose what we want to share with those closest to us. In friendly soul ties, we often share the majority of our secrets and extend the bulk of our trust. In romantic soul ties, we choose what we want to share with our spouses, but all too often, we don't share as much with our spouses as we do our friends. The reason for this is the average married person fears that their darkest and innermost secrets could ruin their marriages. Of course, when we share more with our friends than we do with our spouses, we end up with strong friendships but weak marriages.

Emotional soul ties can be good, but then again, they can be the open door for evil. For example, I once counseled a married woman (we'll call her Melissa) who said she was tired of her husband. I'd spoken with Melissa a few times before, but she'd never spoken as if the marriage was doomed. When she'd said that she was tired of her husband, I noticed how she relentlessly spoke evil of him as if she was building her case against him. I listened intently, and when I saw the opportunity to speak, I cut in. "Who is he?" I asked. Melissa was caught off guard. "Who is who?" she responded. "Who is the guy you're cheating with?" I asked. Melissa was surprised. After all, she hadn't mentioned any guy to me, but she knew that God had revealed her secret to me. With that, Melissa began to confess speaking with another man she referred to as her "friend". She went on and on, telling me about Marquis and how great of a friend he'd been to her, but then, interrupting her brag session to tell me that they'd never had sex. She boasted that he'd never attempted to have sex with her, and he'd been mentoring her regarding her marriage. Of course, I was honest with her and made it very clear that her "friend" was not a friend at all. He was a wolf in sheep's clothing. Marquis was turning Melissa's heart away from her husband, but she had been so caught up in his words and the way he presented himself that she could not see this. You see, they had never had sex (according to her), so their soul tie was emotional. Melissa knew of her husband's imperfections, but Marquis presented himself as a man of all men; a perfect gentleman who understood what that "boy" she was married to was doing wrong. Marquis disguised himself as a friend, but Marquis was a sly devil. After I explained to her why she felt so hostile towards her husband and how Marquis was preying on her, she agreed to stop talking to Marquis.

Melissa's case is not a segregated one. I've met many married men who have befriended women, and these women posed as their understanding friends. They turned to these women when they had disagreements with their wives, but little did they know, they opened themselves up to adulteresses, or better yet, she-devils. An adulteress's Satanic assignment is to destroy marriages, just like an adulterer's Satanic assignment is to destroy marriages. I've seen well-meaning guys fall into the snares placed before them by cunning women who pretended to be their friends. When I was unsaved, morally bankrupt and broken, I hung around women whose sole focus was to nab married men, and their jobs weren't difficult. They looked for married men who weren't guarded by the Word of God, men who trusted in their own abilities to remain faithful to their wives. They gave them listening ears, encouraging words, and comforting hugs. Before long, many of those men were "falling" in love, falling for the lies and falling into the snares Satan had placed before them. Those guys thought they had found what they wanted in a wife, but they hadn't found those qualities in their own wives. Instead, they found them in the adulteresses who pretended to be their friends.

Adulterers and adulteresses want sexual and emotional soul ties with their prey because most adulterers want to separate the people in the marriages they're attacking. Make no mistake about it... an adulterer or an adulteress is nothing more than an attack against a marriage. People who go after married couples know that there are some people who are determined to remain faithful to their spouses, and then, there are some people who are led by the lusts of their flesh. If an adulterer or an adulteress discerns that a person is attempting to remain faithful, they will likely try to establish an emotional soul tie with that person. Emotional soul ties allow predators to wear masks of humility and good intentions until their prey has lowered their defenses.

Another soul tie that can be ungodly is the relationship between a person and his/ her church's leader or members. A religious, emotional soul tie can be ungodly when a church's leader or members uses a person's fear or reverence of God to manipulate, control, seduce or rob them. It goes without saying that if God isn't involved in the relationship, it is an ungodly relationship. Today, there are many church buildings that are being headed up by ungodly leaders, therefore, any relationship or tie those leaders have with the members of their congregations will be labeled ungodly.

I once had a girl reach out to me on Facebook. She wrote me a frantic note, telling me about some man who was a member of the church she attended. The man was someone she trusted, respected and thought highly of, but that all changed the moment he said to her that God told him she was to be his wife. In her note, she told me that she wasn't at all attracted to the guy. She was devastated by the news that she was supposed to be his wife. Of course, I told her that the man was practicing witchcraft by lying to her. God would never force a person to be with someone they are not attracted to, and at the same time, God will always tell you His plans for your life before He tells someone else. If a person tells you God's plans for you and God hasn't shared those plans with you, please know that he or she is likely practicing blatant witchcraft. There are many false prophets in this world, and we have to be aware of their devices.

There has been a recent surge of men approaching women, claiming God told them that those women were to be their wives. This devilish tactic has worked on a few women, but thankfully, the large majority of women who've been approached this way knew better. Of course, these guys are attempting to establish emotional, ungodly soul ties with the women they are trying to coerce down the aisle.

Lastly, two Godly people can have an ungodly soul tie with one another. A good example is the soul tie between a leader and the member of that leader's congregation. The soul tie is Godly if the leader follows the instructions of God as they relate to His sheep, but the soul tie can be ungodly if the leader allows the member to praise or reverence himself or herself. It can also become ungodly if the member begins to have an unnatural affection towards his or her leader. For example, if a member becomes too dependent on his or her leader, that soul tie can easily become an ungodly one. Another example is if the member becomes so reverential towards the leader that he or she exalts that leader above God. In such relationships, the member will almost always become the servant of the leader, and as such, will base his or her decisions and convictions on that leader's opinions. If the leader does not correct this behavior, God will make an open show of the leader, meaning, He will show the member that the leader is human. One of the ways to remind a human that another person is human is to humble or humiliate the person they are exalting. You'll notice that both "humble" and "humiliate" start with "hum", meaning, they are derivatives of the word "human". A good example is if a member has witnessed their leader working in signs and wonders, and they begin to reverence their leaders as the ones performing those miracles. The member himself becomes sick and goes before the leader to be healed. The leader has no healing power; his ability to heal comes from God.

After much prayer, the member goes to the doctor and discovers that he is still sick, and what's worse, the doctor suddenly tells the individual he has three to six months to live. He returns to his leader baffled because he's witnessed people get their healing, but the leader is unable to help him. What has happened is the member has humiliated himself before God and others by reverencing his leader. The leader was humbled by not being able to perform the miracles he's so accustomed to performing. Both people were reminded that they are human, and as such, they need God to perform miracles for them.

Sexual soul ties and emotional soul ties are both dangerous when they are ungodly. One ungodly soul tie can ruin a man's life, finances, relationships and future. That's why it's important to ask the Lord to sever all ungodly soul ties in your life, and then, work tirelessly to remain free of ungodly soul ties. Please know that any and everyone Satan sends into your life is going to attempt to establish a soul tie with you, one way or another. That's why we have to always be watchful and discerning, and we need to always guard our hearts.

Proverbs 4:23 (NLT): Guard your heart above all else, for it determines the course of your life.

Body, Spirit and Soul

Every human being is comprised of a body, a soul and a spirit. A human's soul is comprised of his mind, will and emotions. The soul is the central point between the body and the spirit. It communicates to the spirit of the human whatever we allow to enter our minds. The body often communicates to the soul that whatever it's allowing into it is good, so the soul takes what's given to it and hands it to a man's spirit. Our spirits will then accept or reject whatever the soul is introducing to it. That's why God told us to guard our hearts. The heart of a man, biblically speaking, is his belief system or subconscious mind. *Of course, when I say "man", I'm referring to humans and not just the male gender. Both men and women are considered to be forms of men; thus man and wo<u>man</u>.*

Our belief systems are linked to our minds, but our minds don't automatically believe every piece of information that enters them. Instead, we take what we hear and see, and we measure it against what we've heard, what we're considering, what we've experienced and what we've already believed. We then determine if the information we're considering is truth or lies (to us). If we're unsure about it, we file it away as a question. The Bible tells us to cast down imaginations and every high thing that exalts itself against the knowledge of God (see 2 Corinthians 10:5). The reason we are told to cast down anything that rises against the knowledge (or Word) of God is because whatever we allow to form in our minds is attempting to enter our belief systems. Anything we meditate on for too long will begin to find its way and filter itself into our belief systems through a practice called reasoning, whereas, we'll take the new information, mix it with our personal beliefs, and come up with our own theories. That's why the Bible tells us to "lean not to our own understanding" (see Proverbs 3:5). We will then accept these theories as truth. Once we accept something as true, we've allowed that thing to enter our hearts, meaning, it now has access to our souls, and as such, will begin to wage war against our spirit men. Whenever we allow the truth in, the truth feeds, encourages and strengthens our spirit man against our flesh. Whenever we allow lies in, those lies feed, encourage and strengthen our flesh, and any person who walks after the flesh is walking contrary to God.

There are different types of soul ties. There are Godly and ungodly soul ties, just as there are sexual and non-sexual soul ties. Some (ungodly) soul ties are formed through sexual immorality, while others are formed through ungodly associations. Of course, the strongest of those souls ties are formed through sex. That's because sex allows a person to bypass our belief system and directly form a soul tie with us, whereas, everyone else has to go through a process of being tried and discerned. For example, let's say that you are a woman working at a local pizza joint. One of your co-workers is a woman named Miranda, and Miranda seems eager to be your friend. She's always following you around at work, helping you with your duties, and telling you about her personal life. If you're like most women, you won't immediately trust Miranda. You'll question why she wants to be close to you, and you'll attempt to answer that question yourself by studying Miranda's behaviors. If you're currently involved in a romantic relationship, you will pay attention to Miranda's behaviors and body language whenever your significant (or insignificant) other is around. If you're not in a romantic relationship, you'll listen intently for any motives that Miranda may have for trying to invite herself into your life. Nevertheless, if you were to meet a man (we'll call him Bob), and after a month of dating, you were to sleep with that man, it is because you have decided that you know enough about him to draw what you believe to be a reasonable conclusion about him and the direction of your relationship with him. Once you lie down with him, you've automatically established a soul tie with him, and because of this, you will likely accept a lot of what he says as truth, rather than questioning or trying it. If your heart is hardened by unforgiveness and unsevered soul ties, you won't easily believe Bob, but that does not stop Bob from influencing your life. The moment you slept with Bob was the moment he became the most influential part of your life.

Our Bodies

Remember, your soul is a combination of your mind, will and emotions. Whatever you allow into your subconscious mind will determine the condition of your soul, whether it be declared righteous or wicked. The body, on the other hand, is always going to desire evil because of its sin nature. The flesh is full of wickedness and that's why God told us to not be led by our flesh. You'll notice that your flesh will always desire what it does not need, but will abhor whatever it does need. For example, our bodies crave unhealthy foods, and that's why it's hard to transition from an unhealthy lifestyle to a healthy lifestyle. Our bodies crave sex, even when we're not legally married. Our bodies can crave alcohol, drugs and anything we allow in them, and that's why it's important that we be careful what we put in them.

Whenever we enter ungodly soul ties, our bodies will oftentimes burn with desire. This desire (for many) can be almost unbearable. Of course, this desire is called lust. Lust feels a lot like love, but lust and love are not one in the same. In lust, our bodies will burn with passion and we understand that if we want to quench this desire, we have to engage in some type of sexual immorality. The spirit of a person desires to do what is right by God, but the flesh and the spirit are constantly at war with one another.

Galatians 5:17: For the desires of the flesh are against the Spirit, and the desires of the Spirit are against the flesh, for these are opposed to each other, to keep you from doing the things you want to do.

Our spirits and our bodies belong to God, but here's the thing. We have to rededicate our bodies to God because we were taken into captivity by sin, but we are redeemed by the blood of Jesus (Yeshua) Christ. Our bodies are accustomed to sinning, and therefore, our bodies crave sin with such a passion that it is impossible for us to overcome the lusts of the flesh without the Holy Spirit. Anytime I come across a wife who's complaining about her adulterous husband, I listen intently as she tells me what she wants from him. She wants him to stop cheating, she wants him to be faithful, and she wants him to love her the way she loves him. Nevertheless, it is difficult for her to understand that her husband first needs salvation (if he isn't saved) and the infilling of the Holy Spirit, otherwise, like a dog returns to its vomit, he will return to his adulteries. He needs more than just a changed mind; he needs deliverance! Without deliverance, he will wrestle against the strength of his own flesh versus the weakness of his convictions. The unquenchable and fiery desires of his flesh will continue to rise up against him until he feeds his lusts or he learns to ignore them. Like a drug addict in rehab, he will repeatedly battle with the demands of his flesh and the dark thoughts that will continually visit his unchanged mind. Before long, he will decide that it's easier (and more pleasurable) to give in to his flesh than it is to be the man his wife is begging him to be. The soul ties he has with other women will directly affect his soul (mind, will and emotions). He will remember his rendezvouses with the women he is still soul tied to, and these memories will help to ignite the lust in his flesh. That's where his will then comes in. Even though he knows he is hurting his wife, his flesh will battle with his spirit, and if he doesn't have the Word of God in him like he should, his flesh will continually win that war. He will then will himself into the very sin that's trying to destroy him and his marriage. He may become double-minded, meaning, one part of him wants to be faithful to his wife and he may even try to do so, but another part of him will desire to fulfill the lusts of his flesh. At the same time, it's not always the lusts of the flesh that leads to adultery. Sometimes, men and women commit adultery because of voids, unfulfilled expectations, and a warped sense of reality. For example, in some countries, communities and families, it is expected for the men to commit adultery against their wives. When I was married to a Cameroonian man, for example, his sister tried to convince me that all men cheated. She said that when (not if) my husband cheated on me, I needed to "cover my eyes and know that I am the wife." She was basically saying that I was the most important woman in his life, and as such, I should be honored (insert eye roll here). In other words, any other woman would serve as a concubine. Of course, I didn't agree to this, but the reality is... she was taught, or somehow came to believe that it is a man's instinct and his right to cheat on his wife. The problem, in her warped sense of reality, was not with the cheating man. It was with a woman who wasn't okay with her husband's adulteries; a woman who, by her own understanding, put her marriage at risk by demanding that her husband remain faithful to her. Such a woman was unrealistic and did not realize (or took for granted) how "lucky" she was to have a husband. I can't wholeheartedly say that this was a cultural mindset, but what I can say is that I met a lot of Cameroonian women who thought like her. It could be a village mindset, a tribe mindset, a family mindset, or a mindset she picked up because of her own personal experiences.

Our bodies are nothing more than our houses; after all, we are not our bodies. We are spirits living in bodies, and we have to have a natural body to live in a natural environment. That's why it's illegal for demons to walk the earth, and that's why demonic spirits like to possess human bodies. Nevertheless, demonic spirits want access to our souls where they can influence our mind, will and emotions. That's why people who open their lives to demonic spirits through witchcraft, paganism, occultism and any other demonic access doors are oftentimes filled with murderous or suicidal thoughts. The spirits in or leading them will use them to attack, seduce and destroy the lives of others. Once a demon (or legion of demons) has had its fun using a person, it will discard that person's body like a trash bag. Demons don't love the people they use; they hate them just as much as they hate the people they cannot use.

When our bodies die, our spirits simply leave

our bodies behind. This is similar to a man living in a house. When the man is not home, he will likely leave the lights off, and without him, that house can do nothing on its own. When the man enters the house, the house is now considered to "have life in it" even though the house, itself, is not living. The same goes for the body. Our spirits are the life forces of our bodies, and if the spirit leaves the body, the body, like a house, can settle and make noises, but it cannot do anything of its own. In other words, we are not the creatures we see in the mirror. Instead, we are spirits burrowing in earth suits like snails burrow themselves in shells. The type of suits we wear (gender-wise) determines our roles and responsibilities in earth as assigned by God. Now, you'll notice that many people (mainly homosexuals) believe they were born in the wrong bodies, but this is impossible. How so? Some would say that God doesn't make mistakes, and even though this is true, we must remember that God is perfect, and therefore, can only create perfection. But, wait. How can this be, seeing that some children are born deformed, diseased, or mentally incapacitated? The reality is... God is perfect, but it was sin that deformed us. That's why God said we have to be transformed by the renewing of our minds. When Jesus and His disciples were out ministering one day, they came across a man was born blind. The Jews understood that many children were born with infirmities and diseases because of their parents' iniquities, but they hadn't considered that there could be another reason behind a child's infirmity. That's why Jesus's disciples asked Him who was responsible for the man's blindness. Jesus then informed them that the man wasn't blind because of his parents' sins; God had allowed him to be born blind so that God could get the glory from his healing. Some people would think that this was cruel, but it wasn't. We have to measure natural life against eternal life. God would much rather complicate someone's natural life than to lose that person's soul for eternity. God allowed the man to be blind because He knew that many of His people who had natural sight were blinded to the truth. He knew that if they saw a man who they all knew had been blind since birth receive his sight, many of them would believe upon Him and get saved. As human beings, we often see the one person who's being affected, but God sees the bigger picture because He created it. For example, if you don't know my testimony, I was molested innumerable times as a child. I was physically and repeatedly raped at ten years old by a thirteen year old neighbor, and I lived an agonizing life. As a matter of fact, there are people who find it difficult to believe my testimony because it's hard to fathom that so many wicked things could happen to one person, especially if that person still has his or her sanity. I grew up in a dysfunctional home where I pretty much lived in fear because our house was open to family members (and their demons). I was ridiculed, persecuted, laughed at, talked about, rejected, bullied, molested, raped... you name it. Nevertheless, of everything that happened to me, God never allowed my spirit to be broken. Nowadays, I take what has happened to me and help thousands of broken women get past the demons that have tormented them. You see,

God did not bring the evil that came upon me, but He allowed it because He knew that He was going to use me someday. He knew that there would be many raped, molested, rejected, persecuted, hated and ridiculed men and women who would need to hear my testimony. He knew that I would find my way back to Him, and then, I could point others in His direction. In other words, God sometimes allows bad things to happen to good people because He wants to bless them to be a blessing. Of course, one of the greatest strongholds Satan has brought upon this nation and the church is self-pity. Self-pity is a form of pride, and it pretty much keeps a person from ever overcoming the sins that had been committed against them, thus, causing them to live the rest of their lives as victims.

God knew that I would one day be saved, and He knew that I would dedicate my body, soul and spirit back to Him. He knew that I would forgive those who hurt me because He equipped me with the wisdom to overcome, the strength to forgive and the understanding I needed to keep me free. At the same time, God knows that there are many, many people who will not receive ministry from ministers who haven't suffered many of the afflictions they've suffered in their lives. After all, a person who doesn't have much of a testimony may sometimes come off as self-righteous, judgmental and insensitive. A great example comes from an experience I had with a young woman who was the victim of abuse. Her husband had physically and mentally abused her, and she was looking for a way out. When I spoke with her, one of the very first things I did was share my testimony. When she found out that I had once been married to a man who physically abused me, she opened up and began to tell me what she was going through, but not before telling me that other ministers had tried to speak with her, but she couldn't open up to them. She said that they didn't understand what she was going through because none of them had ever been in an abusive relationship. God was able to reach her through me because I'd been where she was and I had been set free. Sure, being in an

abusive marriage (or relationship) is a
nightmare in itself, but honestly, if I had the
chance to change my story, I wouldn't. The
reason is I wouldn't be able to reach the people
I can reach today. God took what was meant
for evil and turned it around for my good and
His glory.

1 Corinthians 6:19: Or do you not know that
your body is a temple of the Holy Spirit within
you, whom you have from God? You are not
your own, for you were bought with a price. So
glorify God in your body.

When a body is soul tied to another person,
that body will sometimes crave that particular
person; that is, if the mind (one facet of the
soul) isn't against them. You can be soul tied to
a person that your mind, body and soul want
absolutely nothing to do with. Being at odds
with someone doesn't sever the soul tie; it
simply helps you to change your mind about
them. When you became one flesh with that
other person, you joined yourself to them and
the only someone who can separate two souls
is God, Himself. We can only separate our

bodies from one another, but we don't have the power or the tools to separate our souls from the people we've tied them to. In other words, soul ties are almost irreversible; that is, if it wasn't for the blood of Jesus. Of course, we have to repent and ask God to divorce us from everyone we've married through our sexual immorality, and then, we must work at remaining free.

Our Souls

The Greek word for "soul" is "psuche", which translates as being "breath". The KJV New Testament Greek Lexicon (Strong's Concordance 5590) defines soul as:

- *The seat of the feelings, desires, affections, aversions (our heart, soul etc.).*
- *The (human) soul in so far as it is constituted that by the right use of the aids offered it by God it can attain its highest end and secure eternal blessedness, the soul regarded as a moral being designed for everlasting life.*

- *The soul as an essence which differs from the body and is not dissolved by death (distinguished from other parts of the body).*

Genesis 2:7 (KJV): And the LORD God formed man of the dust of the ground, and breathed into his nostrils the breath of life; and man became a living soul.

God took the dirt from the ground and created a man whom He named Adam, nevertheless, before He breathed life into Adam, Adam was nothing but a heap of living dirt. He was a creature, meaning, he was a created thing or creation, and he was alive, but he did not have everlasting life. The life God breathed into Adam was everlasting life. Adam was a soul, meaning, he could live, function and breathe in the realm of the earth, but God made man an everlasting creature by breathing the breath of life into man. He essentially gave mankind His likeness and His abilities.

In reading the text, we see that the author

specifically tells us that the man became a living soul. This would imply that the formed man had a soul (mind, will and emotions), but there was something missing that kept man from being like God. What was missing in man was a spirit, or better yet, an everlasting life force. The word "life" comes from the Hebrew word "chai", which means to be quickened or made alive. Again, what God gave mankind was a spirit. This tells us that before God gave Adam life, he had a mind, a will and emotions (soul), but he did not have an eternal person. This means he was limited to the earth alone, but God wanted man for Himself for eternity, so He gave us all eternal persons called spirits. When Adam and Eve sinned, they fell under the judgment God had judged Satan and his angels by. Satan and his angels are spirits, and God had already declared judgment on evil spirits, meaning, spirits that had sinned against Him. When Adam and Eve sinned, they automatically fell under this judgment. That's why the Bible says that hell was reserved for Satan and his angels. God never intended for mankind to go to hell. Because of sin, Adam and Eve, in a sense, became the living dead since death was already declared upon any spirit found in sin. They brought death into mankind, and every human who was born of the couple would automatically be filled with sin, since we produce after our own kind. This is why God sent His only begotten Son, Jesus Christ. Jesus had to remain perfect to offer Himself as a living sacrifice for anyone who would believe on Him. By accepting Jesus Christ as our Lord and Savior, we received the blessings reserved for Christ Jesus through His righteousness, and He took our sins in His own body. This meant that He had to offer His body as a sacrifice, since the wages of sin is death, but the gift of God is everlasting life through Christ Jesus. When He came out of His body, He was and is righteous, therefore, sin could not keep Him in the grave. At the same time, by believing in Him, we accepted Him as our Lord (Master) and Savior (Salvation), and therefore, we receive His righteousness. Nevertheless, even though our souls are now saved, our bodies are still sin-sick.

The Holy Spirit of God quickened, or made

alive, our spirits. Jesus reconciled us to God, and the Holy Spirit returned to us what sin had stolen from us.

Our souls desire whatever we feed it the most. If we indulge in sin, our souls will crave sin. If we repeatedly feed the Word of God to our souls, our souls will want more of God. In other words, our souls will always stand in agreement with our strongest points. If our flesh is stronger than our spirits, our souls will be led by our flesh. If our spirit man is stronger than our flesh, our souls will be led by our spirits. We can desire to do what is right, but if our strength is found in our flesh, we will be led by our flesh. That's why it's important that we read, study and meditate on the Word of God daily, otherwise, our flesh will grow stronger and rise up against us. We are not our flesh. Please know that when you pass away, your spirit man will leave your body. Your spirit man is your eternal person. The body will then begin to decompose because there is no life left in it to sustain it.

Our Spirits

Our spirits always desire to do what is right. This is namely because the spirit of a man is the one part of him that Satan cannot touch or corrupt. Our spirit man is the part of us that directly communicates with God.

The Greek word for "spirit" is "pneuma". According to Strong's Concordance, the word "pneuma" means "wind, breath, spirit." What is the spirit of a man? The spirit is the everlasting life that God has given each person. It is the very breath of God.

Genesis 2:7 (KJV): And the LORD God formed man of the dust of the ground, and breathed into his nostrils the breath of life; and man became a living soul.

In Genesis 2:7, we come to understand that man became a living soul after God breathed the breath of life into him. This means that man was a soul the moment he was created, but he became a living soul once God breathed the breath of life into him. Some interesting truths to consider are:

- **Man has a spirit, but is a soul.** What does this mean? After all, how can the soul of a man be the essence of that man, seeing, as it is, that the spirit of that man will live forever? It's simple. The soul is the mind, will, and emotions; it is the bridge between the body of a man and his spirit. The spirit is the everlasting force in us that makes us like God; it is the very breath of God and the part of us that can communicate with God. It is our spirits that will return to God, but for the unsaved, it is the body and the soul that will spend eternity in hell (see Matthew 10:28). Why won't people die in hell? Because there will be no more death. Death will also be tossed into the lake of fire. When Adam and Eve sinned against God, they forfeited their right to live with God, because God cannot look upon sin. God is Spirit and when mankind sinned against Him, He had to send mankind out of the place He designed for them to live forever: the Garden of Eden. In other words, human beings became ungodly, or better yet, un-God-like. That's why Christ had to come. He redeemed our souls from hell, but the Holy Spirit quickened our spirits, meaning, we have been restored or reconciled to God.

Scriptural References

Ecclesiastes 12:7 (KJV): Then shall the dust return to the earth as it was: and the spirit shall return unto God who gave it.

John 4:24 (KJV): God is a Spirit: and they that worship him must worship him in spirit and in truth.

Matthew 10:28 (KJV): And fear not them which kill the body, but are not able to kill the soul: but rather fear him which is able to destroy both soul and body in hell.

Acts 2:27 (KJV): Because thou wilt not leave my soul in hell, neither wilt thou suffer thine Holy One to see corruption.

- **We are not our bodies!** The average person looks in the mirror and thinks he or she is the reflection standing in the mirror. This isn't true. We are spirit beings living in bodies. It is our bodies that give us the license to live in the realm of the earth, but once we die, our spirits will separate from our bodies and return to God if we are saved. Those who are not saved will go before God to be judged, but it is their souls that will reside in hell for eternity because their spirits were never quickened, since they did not receive the infilling of the Holy Spirit.

Scriptural References

2 Corinthians 5:8 (KJV): We are confident, I say, and willing rather to be absent from the body, and to be present with the Lord.
Acts 2:31 (KJV): He seeing this before spake of the resurrection of Christ, that his soul was not left in hell, neither his flesh did see corruption.

- **Our spirits communicate directly with God**, but our natural prayers have to be sent up through Jesus. Let's always remember that God is Spirit. When we understand this, we'll better understand how to communicate more effectively with Him. Our soulish prayers go through Jesus when we send them up in Jesus name, but when we pray in the Spirit, our prayers go directly to God.

Scriptural References

Romans 8:2 (KJV): Likewise the Spirit also helpeth our infirmities: for we know not what we should pray for as we ought: but the Spirit itself maketh intercession for us with groanings which cannot be uttered.

1 Corinthians 13:1 (KJV): Though I speak with the tongues of men and of angels, and have not charity, I am become as sounding brass, or a tinkling cymbal.

John 14:13-14 (KJV): And whatsoever ye shall ask in my name, that will I do, that the Father may be glorified in the Son. If ye shall ask any thing in my name, I will do it.

Understanding Our Bodies, Spirits and Souls

What we do in our bodies will determine our souls' eternal homes. Of course, we all know that we will either live in heaven or hell. That's why Apostle Paul told us to glorify God in our bodies. Again, this is to say that we are not our bodies, but our bodies are our spirit man's houses.

The soul of a man communicates with the spirit of that man. It is the soul that will be declared good or evil because the soul is where our will is. We have the power to choose right or wrong, and anytime a man chooses darkness over light, that man has chosen to use his God-given will to sin against God. After a while, his mind will be flooded with dark thoughts and his body will be haunted by unyielding lusts. Once his thinking has been darkened, he will become a dark soul. *Again, this isn't gender-specific. When I said man, I do mean man and woman.*

The body often triggers imaginations, and any time an imagination enters our minds, that imagination is attempting to make itself a part of our subconscious mind. This means it is applying to be a part of our belief systems.

Our minds have three levels: subconscious mind, conscious mind, and unconscious mind. **The unconscious mind** is the most important part of our minds because it controls our breathing, heartbeat, bodily functions, etc. This is the part of the mind that pretty much runs on memory. It is the survival part of our minds. **The conscious mind** is our mind's filter. This is where imaginations take place. We analyze our thoughts from here, and decide whether we will allow whatever we're thinking about to become a part of our subconscious minds. The Bible tells us to cast down imaginations and every high thing that exalts itself against the knowledge of God. We do this with our conscious minds, and we do this by believing the Word of God and not believing anything that is contrary to the Word of God. Anytime we refuse to believe something, we are casting it out of our conscious minds and denying it entrance into our subconscious minds (belief systems). Nevertheless, when we don't cast down imaginations, they enter into our subconscious minds and form themselves into beliefs. When a thought becomes a belief, it can no longer be cast down; it has to be tried by the truth and cast out.

The subconscious mind is where our knowledge, beliefs, habits, and experiences are stored. This is the part of our minds that directly affect our lives because our beliefs will always determine our directions in life. Whatever we believe, we become. Whatever we become, we teach our children to be. In other words, our beliefs are contagious. This is why Satan loves the workings of the subconscious mind. He knows that if he can get lies into our subconscious minds, we will then take those lies and share them with others, including our children (examples: racism, paganism, ungodly traditions, fear, etc.). Additionally, our beliefs will determine what we receive in life. For example, poverty isn't a physical condition; it's a mindset. People who've grown up in poverty grow up with different mindsets (in most cases) than people who've grown up in prosperity. People in poverty need their money to survive, but the money of a prosperous person needs that person to thrive. That's because a prosperous man (or woman) understands the principles of sowing and reaping, even though, in modern day terms, sowing is referred to as investing. Someone with a poverty mindset thinks more along the lines of getting money to spend it. That's because prosperous people and impoverished people have different belief systems. If you are a slave to poverty, you will look for free money because you'll think it's easy money. Poverty breeds opportunists, whereas, prosperity breeds opportunities. It's all just mindsets. For this reason, Satan is always trying to attack, influence and change our subconscious minds.

The subconscious mind is referred to as the heart (biblically speaking).

Proverbs 23:7: For as he thinketh in his heart, so is he.

Unequally Yoked

2 Corinthians 6:14: Be ye not unequally yoked together with unbelievers: for what fellowship hath righteousness with unrighteousness? And what communion hath light with darkness?

Why does the Lord tell us to not be unequally yoked with unbelievers? After all, the average woman thinks she can choose her own man, marry him, and then, raise him up as a man of God. Of course, such marriages are often doomed from the beginning, and those women come to better understand why God says we should not yoke ourselves to unbelievers. First, let's explore the word "yoke". Google's Online Dictionary defines "yoke" as:

- *a wooden crosspiece that is fastened over the necks of two animals and attached to the plow or cart that they are to pull.*

Let's think about two ox around the same

height, wearing yokes that link them together. Both animals, while constricted, can move about easily as long as they are in agreement as to which direction they ought to go in. Nevertheless, if the animals are not in agreement, they will pull on and resist one another, making the journey or the job lengthier and more painful. The same goes for marriage. Anytime a believer marries an unbeliever, both spouses have already entered what the Bible refers to as "a divided home" because they are not in agreement. This means that the two will not cleave together as a husband and wife should cleave, but they'll work against one another. Their souls will be tied, but those ties will serve as yokes, making the journey together very painful. How so? Remember, the soul of a man (and woman) is comprised of the mind, will, and emotions. What's in an unbeliever's mind? According to the Bible, an unbeliever's heart is filled with foolishness. What's on a believer's mind? The Word of God, of course. So, what comes about is a home where two souls who don't agree with one another are now tied to each other.

The unbeliever wants to live life in one direction, while the believer wants to live life in another direction. Instead of advancing forward in life, an unequally yoked couple will oftentimes stop along this journey we call life and fight because they do not agree with one another.

Amos 3:3: Can two walk together, except they be agreed?

Jesus said in John 10:30, "I and my Father are one." What the Lord is saying is not only is He one Spirit with God, but He's on one accord with God. Jesus was and is in no way divided from God, just as a husband and wife should not be divided from one another.

In a home where a couple is unequally yoked, what you'll find is two soul tied people who do not agree with one another. Because of the division, that home will be a place that God rarely visits, unless, of course, one of the spouses repents, submits himself or herself to God and follows His instructions. God lives where there is unity, but Satan thrives in division. Marrying an unbeliever is the same as walking into a marriage with Satan as the middleman. In Godly marriages, God is the third-fold in the cords that are not easily broken. In ungodly or unequally yoked marriages, there is no third-fold, therefore, the marriage is as unstable as a double-minded man. The Bible tells us in 1 Peter 5:8, "Be sober, be vigilant; because your adversary the devil, as a roaring lion, walketh about, seeking whom he may devour." This tells us that Satan cannot devour everyone. It goes without saying that he can devour or divide marriages that are not protected by the God-head. He does this by encouraging division in that home. Satan divides homes by using whichever spouse he has access to, and he entices that spouse to rise up against the will of the other spouse. Again, remember, our souls are comprised of our mind, will and emotions. So, what happens is a couple who is soul tied together will have different plans for their lives, and because they don't think along the same lines, each individual will exercise their individuality instead of coming together in unity. Our minds control our will and our will is influenced by our emotions. In divided homes, you will find souls that are joined together, but are against one another. This is like having an army of men who are supposed to be at war against a conflicting nation, but instead of them warring against their foreign enemies, they begin to war against one another. Their enemies will likely allow them to weaken one another before they attack and destroy them. That's how Satan works! In an unequally yoked home, Satan does not have to attack the couple; instead, he instigates fights by controlling or manipulating whomever he can control or manipulate. He understands that the believer's yoke is going to be heavier and more painful than the unbeliever's yoke because the believer will almost always carry the bulk of the marriage. Think about a yoke between two animals again. What if one of the animals was an ox and the other was a donkey. The ox is substantially taller and stockier than the donkey, therefore, the ox will have to carry the donkey's weight. Of course, this would make the donkey feel "smothered" or "imprisoned", and that's why most unbelievers are the ones to encourage or initiate divorce proceedings against their believing spouses. It's not uncommon for a married unbeliever to say that he or she feels "smothered". Unbelievers can also be heard saying that their spouses are "too clingy", meaning, one person wants to cleave while the other one does not.

Unbelievers want the freedom to sin and that's why they won't give themselves to God. Of course, when I mention unbelievers, I'm also speaking about double-minded believers. They all have commitment issues with God, and will therefore have commitment issues with their spouses.

Note: Just because someone is baptized and is a frequent church attender does not mean they are in one accord with Christ. If a person is romantically interested in an unbeliever, it is because that person is currently double-minded, meaning, they have not settled in their hearts that the Word of God is the final authority. They still think there is a way around the Word that would serve as a shortcut to what they want, but Jesus said, "I am the Way, the Truth and the Life. No one comes to the Father except through me" (See John 14:6). Once we settle in our hearts that the Word of God is truth and there is no other way but through Jesus, our lives will become a whole lot easier. When a couple has not come to understand that the Word is the final authority, they will try to help God fix their lives. They will wrestle against the will of God, all the while, wrestling against one another. They will fight until they either divorce or they finally get in one accord and come to the end of themselves.

What if you are unequally yoked with an unbeliever? First and foremost, let me acknowledge that unequally yoked marriages are nothing short of living nightmares. They involve a lot of mental warfare, and because of this, one of the most important components of human stabilization is often lost and that component is peace. God does tell us how to handle ourselves if we should find ourselves married to unbelievers. First, He told us not to marry unbelievers, but for those of us who did not listen, He gave 1 Corinthians 7:12-16 to help guide us.

1 Corinthians 7:12-16: To the rest I say this (I, not the Lord): If any brother has a wife who is not a believer and she is willing to live with him, he must not divorce her. And if a woman has a husband who is not a believer and he is willing to live with her, she must not divorce him. For the unbelieving husband has been sanctified through his wife, and the unbelieving wife has been sanctified through her believing husband. Otherwise your children would be unclean, but as it is, they are holy. But if the unbeliever leaves, let it be so. The brother or the sister is not bound in such circumstances; God has called us to live in peace. How do you know, wife, whether you will save your husband? Or, how do you know, husband, whether you will save your wife?

Now, this is where things get ugly because this is where most traditional and modern day churches disagree. One church or leader may tell you that it's okay for you to leave your unbelieving husband or wife because your spouse isn't making you happy or performing their roles as spouses. Another church or leader will tell you that it's not okay to divorce your unbelieving husband or wife unless that spouse commits adultery. Honestly, I can tell you that the divide in the church is an emotional one, and one that's brought on by crowds of soul-tied, emotionally unstable individuals who've cried to their leaders that they want out of their marriages. If their leaders did not say what they wanted to hear, they left the church altogether or they went and joined other churches. Many of today's churches and leaders have done the very same thing Moses did. Jesus said that because of the hardness of the people's heart, Moses allowed them to give one another writings of divorcement, but from the beginning, it was not so! Today, many people have hardened their hearts and risen up against the Word of God. This has caused many leaders to revise their teachings to allow what the world refers to as "irreconcilable differences". Nevertheless, after their "divorces", these believers often go out and marry other unbelievers, and then, they run back to the divorce court when their unbelieving spouses behave like the unbelievers they are. They eventually grow tired of their unbelieving spouses, and then, they start looking at the idea of divorce. I know. I used to be one of those believers. The truth is: You can't divorce someone simply because you're tired of them. Jesus said that we have to forgive our brethren (spouses included) seventy times seven, meaning, forgiveness is never to be limited or counted.

Again... it's not okay to divorce your spouse simply because the two of you don't get along. Why is this? Because you likely knew you were unequally yoked before you married that person, but the problem is you successfully manipulated yourself into believing that the marriage would work. You went against the Word of God to enter that marriage, and now, you want to go against the Word of God to exit that marriage.

Is there a way out? Yes, there is, but it can be lengthy and painful. At the same time, you will still need to let God change your mind so that you will change your will and emotions. The way out of an ungodly marriage is as simple as you following the Word of God, even when your flesh wants to do otherwise.

1 Peter 3:1-2: Wives, in the same way submit yourselves to your own husbands so that, if any of them do not believe the word, they may be won over without words by the behavior of their wives, when they see the purity and reverence of your lives.

1 Peter 3:7: Husbands, in the same way be considerate as you live with your wives, and treat them with respect as the weaker partner and as heirs with you of the gracious gift of life, so that nothing will hinder your prayers.

If you're a married woman, the Word tells you to submit yourself to your husband. By doing so, you may win them without having to constantly argue with them. The devil will encourage you to "nag" your husband because the devil will tell you that his change is going to be found in your words, and this is not true. The Word of God says that you ought to submit to your husband so that he can be won over by your behavior. This not only tells us that we can win our husbands over by our behaviors, but our behaviors can cause them to go further in the wrong direction as well. Now, this isn't to encourage anyone to marry an unbeliever because the truth is that more than 90 percent of unequally yoked marriages end in divorce. How do you know, oh woman, whether you will save your husband? You don't! That's the issue. There's no guarantee that he will submit himself to God after you've submitted yourself to him, and that's why God said that if the <u>unbeliever</u> wants to leave, let him depart! What God does is uses the believing spouse to reflect Himself through. He will use the believing spouse to draw the unbelieving spouse, but the unbeliever will ultimately decide if he or she wants to continue towards God or away from Him. If the unbeliever should decide that he or she does not want a relationship with God, that spouse will likely leave, and the Word tells us to let that spouse depart.

For husbands: I find it funny that the Word tells you to "be considerate" of your wives. One of the most common complaints I've heard from married women is how inconsiderate their husbands are. God told men to be considerate because He knows what strengths you have, and He knows that whenever Satan perverts people, He perverts their strength. What then happens is people use their will and their strength to do opposite of what God wants them to do. For example, God has given men the strength to cover their wives and protect their households. Whenever Satan perverts this strength, he encourages or seduces the husband into uncovering his wife by not serving God the way he ought to, and thus, not protecting his household. Such a man may be double-minded, lukewarm and unstable. If his wife is a Godly woman who rebukes him for his behavior, he may consider her to be a "nag", and instead of using his strength to take what he hears and get the wisdom out of it (reflect), he will use his strength to shatter or question what his wife says (deflect).

God also says that the husband is to respect his wife, treating her as the weaker partner and an heir together with himself. What does it mean to treat the wife with respect and as a weaker partner? Again, remember, Satan takes a man's design and perverts him, causing him to go against what God has instructed him to do. The wife is the weaker of the two because God formed man from the dust of the ground, but he took woman from the ribs of a man. In other words, men are God's firstborn. In an unequally yoked marriage, you'll oftentimes see the woman being treated as if she is the stronger of the two. She may be responsible for the upkeep of the home as well as attempting to cover the family with prayer. The man is the first line of defense, meaning, if a thief were to break into the home, the man would first confront and attempt to bind him. If the thief begins to overpower the man, it is the woman's responsibility to get up and assist her husband because "two can withstand him". This works the same way when dealing in the spirit realm. The husband, as the head of his home, should always be the first line of defense against a demonic attack. If a demonic spirit begins to overpower the husband, the wife should always join her husband in the fight. As a matter of fact, when dealing with demonic opposition, a couple is strongest when they operate in unity against the powers of darkness. Nevertheless, when the husband treats the wife as the stronger vessel, he sets her up to be overpowered, overwhelmed and overtaken. This, of course, will cause the house to divide because the wife will begin to lose one of the major components of a successful marriage and that is respect for her husband. After all, how can a wife respect a man who cowers behind her? The Bible says that by not treating your wife as the weaker vessel, your prayers will be hindered.

So, what's the way out? The Word is the way! You simply follow the instructions of God, and continue to strengthen your spirit man by submerging it in the Word of God daily. After you have successfully submitted yourself to God and faithfully (and consistently) honored your spouse the way God told you to, even when your spouse is behaving dishonorably, God will divorce you from your ungodly spouse. But wait! This doesn't mean you will end up in divorce court and separated from the one you love! Instead, God <u>may</u> change your spouse. If and when He does, the person you were once married to (the flesh) will die and God will quicken your spouse through His Spirit. This means your spouse will be a new creature in Christ Jesus, and therefore, he or she will not be the same person you were unequally yoked to. In other words, God can make your marriage a Godly marriage <u>if</u> your spouse <u>chooses</u> to serve the Lord. This means you would be divorced or freed from the person your spouse was, and God will unite you with the new creature that your spouse is. If your spouse should choose to remain the same, God will continue to increase you in Himself. He will lead you, enrich you with wisdom, and guide you to a greater understanding. The closer you get to God, the further you will find yourself getting away from your spouse, but this isn't a bad thing. The unbeliever came into your life because of your disobedience to God, but should the unbeliever choose to leave, it will be because of your obedience to God. This means that the unbeliever has chosen to continue following the Prince of Darkness, and as such, he or she is no longer fit to walk with you. The greater you become in Christ Jesus, the more distant you will be from your ungodly spouse because you will be growing in wisdom, knowledge and understanding, but your spouse will not. The areas you once agreed in may become the areas where you have your greatest disagreements. At this time, you will be strong enough to endure the break if the unbeliever decides to leave. As a matter of fact, you may even welcome the break. This does not mean you did not love your spouse. It simply means you've learned to love God more, and because of this, you've learned to love yourself more. When you learn to love you more, you will want better for yourself.

If you are unequally yoked with an unbeliever, the easiest journey to take is the path as carved out for you by God. Follow the Word and stay on course. There will be times when you will want to get in your flesh to deal with your spouse, but it is never wise to meet a person in a place that you are trying to get them to come out of. Instead, you have to always move to a better mindset; that way, your spouse will either move to a better mindset to relate to you or they'll go ahead and walk out of your life. If the unbeliever wants to leave, you have to let him (or her) depart. In this case, God will permit the divorce (since He's called you to peace), and if you want another shot at love, He will grant you the desires of your heart. Only this time, wait on God for your spouse.

How Soul Ties Affect Us

Satan is always trying to get us to bind ourselves with ungodly soul ties. That's because he knows how the soul behaves when it's tied to someone it shouldn't be tied to. At the same time, what we must all realize is that Satan is not omnipresent, meaning, he is not present in all places at once. He has a lot of demons in his army, and just like God assigns angels to watch over us, Satan assigns specific demons to attack, torment and bind us. Nevertheless, if Satan can get us to bind ourselves, he knows that we will begin to sabotage our own lives and the lives of the people closest to us. So, his demons are always sending people into our lives, and the goal is to get us to soul tie ourselves with these people.

Did you know that the average (legally) married couple would not be married to one another if they hadn't been soul tied to someone else before the marriage? As horrific and unbelievable as this sounds, it's true. Most people choose their mates because of one or more of the following points:

1. **Their spouses treated them better than one or more of their exes-** Believe it or not, there are a lot of people who've been mistreated, misused and mishandled by someone they loved. After spending years of being mistreated, they finally got out of those relationships. When their current spouses came along and treated them better than their exes had treated them, they'd settled it in their hearts that their current spouses were "the one". If they hadn't been treated so poorly by one or more of their exes, they would have likely overlooked or rejected their current spouses.

2. **Their parents accepted their spouses because they were better (in their parents' opinion) than the last people they had romantically linked**

themselves to- This is similar to the first pointer. One of their exes mistreated them, and the parents were ecstatic when their current love interests came along because he or she represented an opportunity for them to love and finally be loved. Their current spouses were probably not "the one" God had chosen for them, but they'd gotten a thumbs up from their in-laws-to-be. After all, in their parents' eyes, their current spouses weren't just opportunities for their sons or daughters to be loved; they were insurance (or roadblocks) that ensured the former lovers would not return or wouldn't be able to return.

3. **Their spouses reminded them of one or more of their exes-** This is so very common with soul tied women. Women tend to go after men who remind them of one or more of their exes, whereas, men tend to avoid women who remind them of their exes... especially if those exes were challenging.

4. **Their spouses were bound by the**

same spirits one or more of their exes were bound by- Familiar spirits attract familiar people because people get comfortable in familiar settings. A good example would be a man who is used to being in relationships with women who have Jezebel spirits. They are comfortable being Ahabs, so anytime they come across women who have Jezebel spirits, they will pursue those women. They demonstrate their abilities to be submissive, passive and loyal Ahabs by continuing to pursue Jezebel even after she's lashed out at them. They're familiar with women who have Jezebel spirits and such men would not be happy if they were married to submissive, Godly women.

5. **Their spouses stood up to one or more of their exes-** Let's say a woman has been abused by one of her exes. She's broken the relationship off and is trying to move on with her life, but her abusive ex keeps calling her, threatening her and showing up at her job. She

meets a man, but isn't completely attracted to him. She tells herself that he is a nice guy and she reminds herself of what happened the last time she chose a guy based on what she wanted in a man. So, she gives in and gives the guy her number, however, she finds herself still not too attracted to him. That is... until he confronts her stalking, unstable ex. She sees him standing up to the guy, and suddenly thinks she's in love with him.

This is very common for women because we like to feel protected, but sometimes, we take this for granted when we're accustomed to living stable, uninterrupted lives. When that security has been taken from us, we then realize the value of feeling secure. When someone comes along and offers us that security again, it is not difficult for us to find ourselves momentarily attracted to that person.

6. **They lived in a below-average or mediocre lifestyle with one of their**

exes, and their current spouses offered them the opportunity for a better life- Example: At a young age, Kristy meets and marries Benjamin, who happens to be one of her co-workers at a local retail store. The couple lives in poverty, and eventually, they divorce when Kristy discovers Ben's infidelities. One day, Kristy meets a well-to-do real estate investor by the name of Lloyd. Lloyd is fifteen years older than Kristy, and she's not attracted to him, but she is attracted to his lifestyle. Kristy marries Lloyd, hoping that one day she will be attracted to him. Had Kristy gone to college and done something with her own life, she more than likely wouldn't have married Ben. She would have been able to afford a better lifestyle for herself, and therefore, she likely wouldn't have married Lloyd either. Additionally, if Kristy had never experienced what it was like to live in poverty with a man, it would have been easier for her to resist Lloyd.

7. **They wanted to make one or more of their exes jealous-** The reality is that there are quite a few people who enter relationships just to make their exes green with envy. They found people who they felt looked better than their exes or people their exes were intimidated by, and they courted these people to get a rise out of their exes. Nevertheless, upon hearing that their exes were getting married to other people or had created children with other people, they took their relationships to the next level.

8. **They had children with one or more of their exes, and their current spouses appeared to be a great fit in the lives of their children-** Most decent parents want their children to have the benefits of a two-parent household. They also want their children to have stepfathers or stepmothers who love and treat them as if they were their own children. When they met their current partners, they noticed how attentive and loving they were to their

children. They also noticed how comfortable their children were with their current spouses, so they married their spouses because they made great stepparents.

9. **Their spouses are the most attractive people they've ever been romantically involved with-** This one is a crime oftentimes committed by men. Not all men, of course, but the ones who aren't used to getting a lot of attention from the opposite sex. It goes without saying that some people are shallow, but the truth is, there are some men (and women) out there who aren't stable enough for serious relationships. Let's say a guy named Hector has been in a relationship with his girlfriend, Maria, for thirteen years. Hector, by society's standards, is an unattractive man, and Maria, by society's standards, is an unattractive woman. One day, Hector finally graduates from law school and lands his dream job, where he meets a secretary named Irene. Irene, by

society's standards, is beautiful and she makes it very clear that she wants to date Hector. After a two month affair, Hector ends his thirteen year relationship with Maria and marries Irene. Now, you may be saying that this has nothing to do with Maria. Hector is just a shallow jerk on the verge of a very important lesson, and you are somewhat right. Nevertheless, the truth is... Hector is comparing both women on the beauty scale, and to him, Maria has lost the beauty pageant. So, he runs off and marries a woman he's only known for two months because he doesn't have a whole lot of experience with women. So, Irene ended up married to Hector simply because she looked better than Maria. If Hector had been single the entire time, he would have likely dated a few women here and there, and he would have recognized Irene for what she was: a gold-digger.

10. **Their spouses were there for them when they'd suffered through**

traumatic breakups from other people- Some couples started off as friends. One of the parties involved was in a relationship with someone else, and the other party was nothing more than a supportive friend. Example: Larry and Tina are close friends, but Tina is in a relationship with Xavier. Tina talks to Larry everyday about Xavier's behaviors, and he helps her through some pretty traumatic events. When Tina's relationship with Xavier ends, she turns to Larry for consoling and Larry is there for her. Before long, Tina finds herself falling for Larry because he's been a great friend to her.

The point is... the large majority of people who are married today are married to the people they've chosen because of someone in their pasts. That's why soul ties are important to the devil. He likes to lock people into types, meaning, they keep dating the same types of people, but in reality, they're simply attracted to certain types of spirits in people.

I know you've heard one of your friends or loved ones refer to another person as cute, and then, without thinking, they said that person reminded them of one of their exes. Before long, they are involved with that person, and once that relationship ends, they find someone else that reminds them of the person they just broke up with. That person is unknowingly attracted to a familiar spirit. A familiar spirit specializes in getting people to feel comfortable around it. Familiar spirits tend to go through family lineages for hundreds, and sometimes, thousands of years undetected because the people who host them don't realize they're bound. They believe that they simply prefer to be around certain types of people, even though the people they feel most comfortable around are the ones who keep abusing, hindering and misusing them. You'll notice, for example, a woman whose daughters have picked up her "love them and leave them" trait with men. Just like their mother, the Jezebels in training are beautiful, witty, arrogant and promiscuous. Some of the guys who end up with them, find themselves smitten with their beauty, charm and nonchalant attitudes. After the relationships are over, those same men will date multiple women, looking for the security they felt when they were with those young women. Anytime they come across decent women, they will mistreat and abandon them because they feel most comfortable with women who have Jezebel spirits. Nevertheless, whenever you hear they've settled down and are about to get married, you'll notice that they've gone out and found women who are about to give them a run for their money (and their sanity). People look at these guys and shake their heads in awe of their simple-mindedness. It's not uncommon to hear people saying things like, "You know, he was dating Cecilia, and she was a really, really nice girl! That girl loved him and he took her through hell! He kept cheating on her, hitting on her, and just being plain ole mean to her! He finally got tired of Cecilia and ended things with her to be with that ole witch he's with now. I don't know what he sees in that girl! She's unfaithful, disrespectful and sassy-mouthed; plus, she loves to fight! He went and got that wicked woman, and now, he wants to marry her!" What does he see in her? He sees himself in her! He sees the demons he's come to love in her! More than likely, he sees the traits of spirits he's not yet familiar with in her, and they are intriguing to him. Of course, he doesn't know he's attracted to spirits; he simply sees something mysterious in her and he wants to try and solve the mystery.

Soul tied men tend to go after women who are even more broken than the women they've soul tied themselves to in the past. That's because men are natural hunters and hunters tend to get bored when they become experts at hunting a certain type of prey. They like to venture off and chase new game, so whenever a man comes across a woman who's a little too much like the women in his past, he will likely bore of her easily. Nevertheless, when a woman comes his way who's unlike any woman he's ever conquered, he'll pursue that woman, not knowing that the demons in him are attracted to the demons in her. Soul tied women tend to go after men who remind them of the guys from their pasts. Women oftentimes get comfortable with a certain type of guy and won't venture too far away from his type. That's because women aren't hunters; they're nurturers, and it's easier for them to nurture what they're familiar with than it is to nurture something that's new to them. For this reason, women tend to get with men they don't trust, but not necessarily because of something their current lovers did. Oftentimes, women don't trust what they see in the eyes of their current love interests because they're familiar with it. Instead of understanding that they are actually identifying demonic traits in a person, most soul tied women will find themselves attracted to the same spirits in different men. Somehow, the enemy is able to convince them that they have the power to tame the wild streak they see in their lovers' eyes. Because of this, many women find themselves learning to master certain types of men, even though they can't tame the spirits therein.

Soul ties affect us in more ways than we realize. They inspire us to choose the life partners we end up with, and they affect our careers, religious views and so on. For example, some women are lawyers today because some of their exes were lawyers and they wanted to prove themselves to those exes. Some men are doctors today because some woman dumped them for a guy she believed to be better than they were, so they went out and worked hard at becoming better off than the guys they'd been dumped for. Additionally, some people went downhill on the career path after they'd been hurt. For example, some men dropped out of college because they were traumatized by breakups. Some women have never realized their full potential because one of their exes told them that they weren't smart enough to be anything other than what they were when they were dating those exes. Some men and women never left the cities or states they grew up in because they didn't want to move too far away from the people they had soul ties with. Again, this is why the enemy is passionate about getting us wrapped up in the wrong relationships. He knows that soul ties are strong enough to keep us from ever reaching our full potential in Christ Jesus. And this is why we have to be more determined to remain free than the devil is determined to bind us or keep us bound.

We must also realize that not all soul ties are established through sexual intercourse. Some soul ties are established through our friendships or associations with other human beings. Remember, David and Jonathan's souls were tied, and they were just friends. As a reminder, the Bible says Jonathan's soul knit with David's soul, but it did not specifically say that David's soul knit with Jonathan's. This is very important because many of us have had friendships where we've loved our friends to the point where we would have done almost anything for them, but they did not have that same love for us in return. Of course, this upset us, and in most cases, we ended the friendships with those people. This is because they were more valuable to us than we were to them, and such friendships are one-sided and only benefit one of the parties involved.

Our soul ties with our friends can be just as life-altering or life-threatening as our soul ties with our romantic interests. That's because our friends, in most cases, have direct links to our subconscious minds. They no longer have to reason with our conscious minds; that is, unless we don't trust them. They have access to our belief systems, and they have an access code called "trust" that allows them to speak effortlessly into our lives. Even though most of us don't accept everything our friends say as true, they still have enough power to make us question ourselves and others. Friends have the ability to sow seeds in our hearts at will.

I remember meeting a girl who I'd initially believed would be a lifelong friend of mine. We seemed to have a lot of similar interests, and we were both believers. It didn't take me long to realize that our friendship was likely not going to survive because I saw a lot of contention in her, and that contention kept bleeding over into our friendship. She would always tell me stories about people she met or worked with, and the large majority of her stories involved her getting into an argument or a heated debate with someone. Nevertheless, I silently hoped she would be better with me, but that just did not happen.

One of the things I heard "Penny" repeatedly say whenever she told me about another argument she had gotten into was that she had sown the seeds she needed to sow in her opponent's mind. Penny was passionate about telling folks what she perceived to be wrong with them, and it goes without saying that she was wrong more times than she was right. However, she was determined to get people to believe about themselves what she believed about them. Penny was led by her perception of other people, and it wasn't long before she was pointing her perception at me and firing away. I had to distance myself from her, but I always remembered her saying that she had sown the seeds she needed to sow. In other words, whether people believed her report or not, her intentions were to get her words into their hearts and hope that those words would eventually produce fruit in their lives. Penny didn't realize it, but she'd readily admitted time and time again that she would get close enough to people to sow seeds in their hearts, and when they wouldn't receive those seeds, she would get into verbal wrestling matches with them. Her goal was to pour out what she had in her heart, and like a mother bird, she would try to force her beliefs down her "friends'" throats. In her mind, she was never wrong. As a matter of fact, she genuinely believed that she was doing everyone a favor, but in truth, Penny was bound by hurt, unforgiveness and soul ties. Just like hurt people hurt people, bound people bind people. She would get close enough to establish soul ties with her friends, and then, she would start unleashing what she had stored up in her heart about them.

The reality is... there are a lot of women (and men) like Penny in this world. When we meet these souls, we see the light in their eyes that Satan has not yet dimmed, but what we should force ourselves to see is the truth. We can't change people; we can only encourage them to change themselves. That is, of course, if they want to be changed. Penny didn't hide who she was from me. I simply saw the good in her, and I saw her contentious ways as nothing more than a lack of understanding, and that's not always a fatal flaw. (Note to the women: One of the issues with us, as women, is we see everyone as fixable, so we try to be friends with any and everyone who has something in common with us, regardless of how many rips we see in their souls. We are loving creatures, but we must always remember that we cannot out-love God, meaning, we can't do for others what they refuse to let God do for them).

Soul ties established through friendships also help set the foundations for the romantic soul ties we enter. How so? Have you ever noticed that we tend to be more concerned about what our friends think of our potential love interests than what we think of them ourselves? Of course, this is especially true for young men and women, not so much for older people. Additionally, the average person is set up at least one time in his or her life by a friend.

Soul ties are real and they do affect our lives, and that's why we have to make sure we ask God to free us from every ungodly soul tie we've ever entered. After that, we must work continuously to remain free.

Soul ties affect:
1. Our identities
2. Our day to day decisions
3. Our career paths
4. Our romantic relationships
5. Our friendships
6. Our self-perception
7. Our self-esteem
8. How we view others
9. How much money we make
10. Our faith
11. Our health
12. Our state of minds
13. Our children
14. Our lives as a whole
15. Our relationship with God
16. Our eternities

Now, we can better understand why it is

important to Satan that we be bound by ungodly soul ties. We can also better understand why God wants us to remain free of ungodly soul ties and associations. When we are free of ungodly soul ties, God can use us without limits. Free yourself from the grips of the enemy today. Ask the Lord to divorce you from every illegal soul tie in your life, and remember to stay free. Once God releases you, the enemy will try to bind you again. Don't let him do this. Stay in the Lord and don't move until He tells you to; that way, He will connect you to the people He has chosen to be in your life, and He will disconnect you from the people Satan has assigned to ruin God's plans for your life. Be free today and stay that way.

Ten Truths About Soul Ties

There are so many fascinating truths to learn about soul ties and how they cause us to behave. Below, you'll find ten interesting truths about soul ties:

1. **We'll trade itches for pain.** Have you ever noticed that whenever your legs, arms or back starts itching, you'll scratch yourself to get rid of the itch? What you've just done is subtly or forcefully distracted yourself by trading that itching sensation for pain. You see, you know how much pain your body can withstand without that pain being bothersome to you, so whenever an itching sensation ignites on your body, you'll trade that itching sensation for pain. You'll notice that sometimes you may scratch yourself a little too hard; the average person prefers subtle pain over itching. Soul ties trigger us in similar

ways. Whenever we're dealing with the pain of a breakup, we'll often mask that pain by entering new relationships. We're always trying to trade one feeling for another feeling, but this only weakens us because God designed us to withstand our broken hearts. Our broken hearts are supposed to teach us how valuable and true the Word of God is, so that we can look at the paths that led us to our broken hearts and compare them to the instructions God has given us in His Word. Most people try to divert their own attention away from their broken hearts by entering new soul ties. This doesn't stop the pain from coming, but instead, delays and intensifies it.

2. **Soul ties take away the innocence of a woman**; the very innocence and child-like behavior that attracts a man to his wife. Have you ever noticed how beautiful a woman appears when she's childlike? I'm not talking about the childlike behaviors of someone who's developmentally delayed; I'm talking

about the innocence associated with having never been hurt or betrayed. Here's the thing: A wife is to always have this innocence about her, but because of unsevered soul ties and past relationships, the average woman projects a strength that most men find repelling. To the women: When we truly repent and ask the Lord to sever every ungodly soul tie away from us, one of the things He restores to us is this innocence. This doesn't mean you'll be "stupid" as some women would say, but it does mean that you won't let your past interfere with your future. When you notice that childlike trust starting to penetrate through the strengths you've developed over the years, you can rest assured that God is prepping you to be found by your God-appointed husband.

3. **You can't be found until you're in position.** Have you ever prepared to take a flight? You'll notice that whenever you're at the airport, you must first check in, check your luggage, go

through security screening, and then, head to your gate. Once you're at the gate, you have to wait for your plane to arrive. This means that if you're not at the gate when the staff starts loading the planes, you will undoubtedly lose your flight and delay your arrival. Here's the thing. Breaking ungodly soul ties is a process that must be completed before you can truly say you're waiting on your God-appointed spouse. If you were to go to the airport and sit in the lobby, you couldn't truly say that you were waiting for your flight because you have not gone through the proper procedures, and as such, the TSA (Transportation Security Administration) won't let you board the plane. You're not even in position to board the plane because it is not going to travel through the airport to get to you. You have to go to it. The average believer finds a comfortable mindset and starts waiting from there. They're soul tied to other people, still bound by unforgiveness and just not in the mindset of a spouse, and because of this, many believers wait years, and sometimes, decades to be found by their God-appointed spouses. They haven't been processed yet! You have to go through the entire process to get to the point where you are truly waiting, otherwise, you'll find yourself waiting in vain and your arrival to your "promised land" will be delayed.

4. **Unforgiveness is the evidence of an unsevered soul tie.** A person who hasn't forgiven another human being is still tied to that person because of their unforgiveness. Think of a debt collection agency and a man who owes that debt collection agency. The agency and the man are tied together until the debt has been paid. The agency will harass, threaten and sue the man until he has paid his debt in full. That's how unforgiveness works. Even if you don't call, email or text the person you've linked yourself to, you're still holding on to that person through your

unforgiveness. This means you think that individual owes you something, even if what you're willing to settle for is an apology. If you don't forgive a person, the soul tie between you and that person cannot and will not be severed on your end.

5. **Unsevered soul ties send us in the wrong directions looking for love.**
   Let's face it... God is love, and there is no greater love than His love. However, we enter ungodly soul ties when we veer off the righteous path and go searching for love outside of God. Once we've entered these soul ties, we go further into sin looking for love, and all too often, we become familiar with a certain type of lover. When this happens, we look for love in certain types of people. God requires that we seek first the kingdom of God and all His righteousness; that way, He can add everything we need and want to us. This includes love, understanding, the freedom to be who we are designed to be and compassion.

When we embrace the immeasurable love of God, we won't go looking for love in man's eyes. Instead, we will let the Author, Creator and the very Essence of Love guide our steps until we meet the individuals God has specifically assigned to our lives. As we follow God, love will lead, follow, cover, surround and fill us.

6. **Soul ties were designed by God to link us to our spouses**, but the enemy perverted the hearts of God's people, and the very ties God designed to help a man cleave to his wife are now being used by Satan to bind God's people in emotional, spiritual and financial bondage. Again, God designed soul ties to link us to our spouses, but Satan uses unsevered soul ties to divide us from our spouses.

7. **Soul ties aren't always established through sex**, even though the most powerful soul ties are established through sexual contact. Remember the story of David and Jonathan. They were

friends and a soul tie was established between them because of their love for one another. Every friend you have has a soul tie with you. That's why Satan works tirelessly to link us to ungodly, unfaithful people. That's also why God said that we are to guard our hearts; after all, soul ties are established in our hearts, and of course, our hearts are the engines of our lives. Even the people we choose as friends can lead or send us in the wrong directions looking for love. For example, we, as human beings, tend to influence one another. You'll notice that whenever you consider romantically linking yourself to another person, you will likely introduce your potential love interest to your friends. After that, you'll either ask for their opinions about your new love interest, or if they're upfront, you'll wait to see what they have to say. Even though we make our own choices, the people closest to us do influence our decisions... whether we want to admit it or not. Oftentimes, God won't allow a man to find his wife or a wife to be found by her husband when those individuals are linked to the wrong people. That's why it's important to not only ask to be freed from ungodly soul ties established through sex, but it is also wise to ask God to deliver us from any and everyone (family included) who is hindering us in any way.

8. **Contrary to popular belief, soul ties don't heal over time**; they have to be severed by God, Himself. Please understand that we were never designed to link ourselves to the wrong people. God designed mankind to obey Him, but sin has perverted our designs, and because of this, we tend to link ourselves to all manners of souls. Every soul tie we have is affecting our lives in one way or another, and that's why we have to repent of all ungodly soul ties and ask the Lord to sever them. The average person thinks soul ties fall off like scabs when their hearts have healed and they've adjusted to life without their

former lovers, but this isn't true. Instead of being freed from the ungodly soul ties, we simply learn to adapt to life without our former lovers. This is oftentimes evident when former lovers unintentionally run into each other at the supermarket, park or at a social event. One or both parties will likely experience a rapid heartbeat, a resurfacing of old emotions, anger, curiosity, or an almost irresistible desire to reconnect. The truth is... soul ties don't heal over time; they have to be severed.

9. **Ungodly soul ties ruin married sex.** A lot of people get legally married in the eyes of the law, while being illegally married in the eyes of God. The reason their marriages are doomed is because they're already married to other folks and they will bring these folks into their marriage beds unintentionally. That's why some people are labeled as "good lovers", while others, are labeled as "not so good lovers". The issue isn't always in

their performance, per se. Oftentimes, the issue is in their inability to identify their current partner's sexual personality, or in layman's terms, they're still sexually in sync with their former lovers, but they haven't identified their current lovers' rhythm. Because of this, many married couples end up in sexless marriages. They don't know why they don't enjoy sex with one another anymore. They enjoyed sex at the beginning of their marriages because, at that time, they were exploring one another's sexual personality, but as time went on, they defaulted to what they knew, or better yet, who they knew. This is why it is absolutely necessary to be delivered from ungodly soul ties before we meet and marry our God-appointed spouses.

10. **People bound by ungodly soul ties don't have sound minds.** This includes those individuals who live what appears to be successful lives. A sound mind is a blessing from God. Please know that sin is not only Satan's attempt to bound and

kill you, but he wants to take away the soundness of your mind because he knows that without it, you are going to self-destruct. Remember, Satan is a thief and a liar, therefore, his main purpose in your life is to steal what God has given you. The easiest way for him to get access to your blessings is to lie to you. If you don't know the truth, you will fall for the lies of Satan and open your heart to him. Once Satan has access to the heart, he will steal your peace, joy and anything else he sees is benefiting your life. He will then download the evils of his heart into yours, and sometimes, he'll leave the keys to success in you so you won't know he's there. Additionally, by "allowing" you to become or remain successful, he knows that others will view the wreck that is your life and think they can live recklessly and still find success. Remember, Satan is strategic in his attacks, so never underestimate him; after all, he has absolutely nothing left to lose, which makes him the most dangerous, despicable and desperate spirit walking the earth today.

Renting Your Soul for Love

Have you ever been approached by a thief in the parking lot of a mall? If you haven't, the event goes a little something like this:

- A suspicious man or woman approaches you. That man or woman looks both ways to ensure no one else is around to witness what they're doing.
- The thief tells you that he or she has some really great deals for cheap. The thief then reveals the merchandise to you. Oftentimes, the stolen goods are in the thief's coat or handbag.
- The thief tells you the price you'll have to pay to purchase the goods.
- If and when you turn the thief down, he or she offers you a better price or a bundle deal.

One of a thief's favorite items to steal is jewelry. It is not uncommon to be approached by thieves selling what they claim to be gold, platinum or sterling silver jewelry. A thief will hand you a gold plated, cubic Zirconia ring and tell you that the gold is real and the diamonds are real. He or she will then offer you that ring for $40, even though the thief claims the ring is selling for over a thousand dollars. If you're silly enough to buy that ring, you'll soon come to find out that a thief is not a respecter of persons. They want what they want and they'll lie, cheat and steal to get it. People who have fallen for this scam have paid, for example, forty bucks for a ring that's retailing for ten dollars. They can't call the police because the minute they purchased those rings, they too became thieves. They can't ask the thief for a refund because a thief is a thief. They can't go back and find the people who've victimized them because thieves rarely return to the same spots. They can only take the lesson behind it, and hopefully, learn from it. In other words, a thief can't rebuke a thief.

If a thief approaches you, you must remember that he/she doesn't have anything valuable to offer you, especially if he or she is trying to sell you jewelry. How so? Go into a jewelry store and you'll find that the expensive jewelry is kept locked away behind the counter. The cheap jewelry, on the other hand, is not locked up. The cheap jewelry is easily accessible, and therefore, it's easy to steal. Ordinarily, thieves wouldn't be interested in costume jewelry because costume jewelry is worthless, but nowadays, they steal costume jewelry and pass it off as real diamonds, gold, platinum or silver. They do this because they've found that there are a lot of people who don't mind buying things from thieves, but what these people don't realize is the valuable jewelry is locked away. It's difficult for a thief to get to the valuable stuff!

How does this tie in to soul ties?

1 Corinthians 6:18-20 (ESV): Flee from sexual immorality. Every other sin a person commits is outside the body, but the sexually immoral person sins against his own body. Or do you not know that your body is a temple of the Holy Spirit within you, whom you have from God? You are not your own, for you were

bought with a price. So glorify God in your
body.

You'll notice that 1 Corinthians 6 says that you
were bought with a price. What does this
mean? Jesus paid the price for you. He
redeemed you with His shed blood, therefore,
you are no longer a slave of sin. When you
practice sexual immorality, you are delivering
yourself to what Christ has delivered you from.
The thief (Satan) has no intentions to pay the
full price for your soul; after all, he can't afford
you. That's why he has to get you to lower
yourself so that he can reach you. Since you
were purchased by the precious shed blood of
Jesus Christ, Satan can't touch you. Since you
are hidden underneath the wings of God and
locked away in His heart, Satan can't steal you.
So, what's a desperate devil to do? He tempts
you with sin, and to do this, he uses whatever
voids, desires and lusts you have. Imagine that
you were in a parking lot, hiding behind Jesus
while Satan stood in front of Him calling your
name. You are protected by the Lord, Himself,
but Jesus is not going to oppose your will,

meaning, if you choose to go to Satan, He will let you go.

Satan offers you a new car, but you don't budge. He then offers you a better paying job, but you refuse to move. Finally, he looks at you and remembers that you didn't have the best upbringing; after all, he helped your parents raise you. Your parents weren't the loving, doting parents that most children want and need. Instead, they were cold, uncaring, neglectful and abusive. Suddenly, that ole devil looks sympathetic. With tears in his eyes, he offers you something that looks like love and feels like love. The naked eye can't tell the difference, but you're confident that you're being blessed with the opportunity to finally be loved by someone. You don't realize that you're trading the most valuable part of you (your soul) for a cheap, generic imitation of love. Satan hands you a beautifully crafted man who has that same compassionate look in his eyes that his daddy (Satan) has, but this guy comes off as very sincere. After all, we know that Satan is a liar who can't be trusted, but who can turn down a creature who was made in the image of God when that creature wears the mask of humility? This man says all of the right things, and even though he's not in Christ Jesus, he opens his heart and shows you his wounds. Behind all of the wounds and the emotional barbwire, you see what you think is his little black box of love. If you can only get to his black box, you'll know what happened to him. You'll better understand why he is the way he is and maybe... just maybe... you can fix him. Soft music fills the air, the touch of his hands overwhelm you, and the scent of his skin is bewitching. In his eyes, you see your reflection, and you notice that your reflection looks even more beautiful and vibrant in his eyes than it does in the mirror. You get lost in the idea of spending your life with him. You get lost in the idea that you can help that beautifully designed man to heal the wounds in his heart. Satan looks at you and says, "He's Christian, too. He just needs a push and he'll serve the Lord with you." Before you know it, you've left the protection of Christ Jesus to join your soul to one of Satan's children. Jesus paid the price for you, but you went back and tried to sell your soul for love. There's a problem with this. You don't belong to you so you can't give yourself away. You can loan yourself to lies, but eventually, the truth is going to stake claim to your soul. What you didn't realize is that Jesus loves you. You were searching for something you already had. You were longing for something that was already yours. So, you end up in a relationship with a crafty, sin-loving guy who builds you up just to tear you down. It isn't long before you realize that the price Satan charged you for that man is far more than what he's worth. You were robbed, but it's not all the devil's fault. You shouldn't have negotiated with the devil to start with, so you can't call heaven and file a report without first having to acknowledge your wrongs. You can't rebuke the devil when he stakes claim to the man you chose for yourself; after all, that man belongs to him. He just loaned him to you, just like you loaned yourself to him. Eventually, a loan has to be returned or repaid <u>with interest</u>.

It is human nature to want to be loved, but the

amazing truth is... most folks who enter ungodly relationships have never truly experienced love. They've experienced what looked, felt and behaved like love, but they don't know what it feels like to be loved by a person who is romantically linked to them. Many of them will leave this earth never experiencing true love. They will have spent their lives renting out their souls for love, but never getting anything valuable in return. The truth is:

→ Many will know what it feels like to be called a husband or a wife, but they won't know what it feels like to be loved by the person they're married to.

→ Many will know what good sex, bad sex and great sex feels like, but they will never experience Eros (romantic) love coupled with Agape (unconditional) love.

→ Many will know what it feels like to be a parent, but they won't know what it feels like to have someone with them to help raise their children... in love.

→ Many will know what it feels like to

invest in love, but they will never see a
return on their investments.

→ Many will know what it feels like to love
someone, but they won't know what it
feels like to receive love in return.

You are valuable to God and that's why He
wants to hide you underneath the shadow of
His wings where the enemy can't touch you.
Don't let the enemy discount you or cause you
to discount yourself. Sure, it may take a while
before someone comes along who can afford
your hand in marriage, but at least they will be
willing to pay the price for you, meaning, they
will know your worth. They will serve God to
have you, just as Jacob served Laban to have
Rachel. A man who works tirelessly to acquire
the things he wants in life won't buy an
expensive piece of jewelry and just leave it
lying around the house. He will put it away in a
safe place because it's valuable to him. The
same goes for a man (or woman) who's
faithfully obeyed and served God and received
one of His rewards: a God-appointed spouse.
They will love, protect and cover their spouses

because they know how uncommon and valuable their spouses are. Someone who has not paid the price for you cannot and will not know your worth.

Musical Soul Ties

For hundreds of years, theologians have
debated whether or not music is linked to soul
ties. At the same time, the church today doesn't
speak a whole lot about soul ties because a lot
of leaders are either uneducated about soul
ties or they're too afraid to teach on such a
controversial subject. After all, when one starts
teaching on sex and soul ties, there is a lot to
be unearthed that goes against some of the
very teachings of our modern day churches. For
example, as I mentioned earlier, there is no
such thing as premarital sex, since the two shall
be one the minute two people sleep together.
It simply becomes fornication because it's out
of order with God, and therefore, considered
sexual immorality. Fornication isn't premarital
sex; it's sexual immorality. Sexual immorality
can be adultery, sex outside the verbal
covenant and Godly order of marriage,
homosexuality and any other sexual behavior
deemed as immoral. This isn't an opinion; it's

biblical. When Christ came across the Samaritan woman, He told her she'd had five husbands, but the guy she was currently with was not her husband, meaning, she hadn't had sex with him yet. Initially, the Samaritan woman had stated that she was not married, and Jesus agreed with her. This means that she was more than likely widowed five times, or she may have been divorced because of Samaritan traditions. You see, Samaritan women were not allowed to speak with men in the streets, especially if the women were married. If their husbands found out that they had been verbally communicating with men on the streets, they could and likely would divorce their wives, since such an act was considered the equivalent of adultery. As a matter of fact, men would close their eyes anytime they came across women in public places. So, the fact that the Samaritan woman actually engaged in conversation with Jesus is telling in itself. She could have possibly been a rebellious woman who freely spoke with men, or then again, she was likely widowed since Jesus agreed with her when she said she didn't have a husband.

Many people today think about the old days using modern day mindsets and modern day traditions, and this leads to a bunch of false doctrines being birthed. Nevertheless, Samaritans were basically half Jews, half Gentiles; whereas, they (or their parents) were once Israelites, but they'd intermarried with Gentiles and began to practice heathenism. Reference.com defines heathenism as:

1. *A belief or practice of heathens; idolatry.*
2. *Barbaric morals or behavior; barbarism.*

Samaritans were once devoted Jews, but they separated themselves from the Jewish faith to practice heathenism. The Samaritans retained many of their Jewish beliefs and traditions, all the while, practicing idolatry. The point is... many don't teach on soul ties because it's not a subject that's been heavily studied, plus, the truths that are unearthed when studying such a controversial topic would make many churches have to change their sermons on sex and marriage. Since sex outside the Godly covenant of marriage is still a form of fornication, many leaders who have studied and found the truth about fornication, premarital sex and the like didn't think it was necessary to clarify the terms. However, it is necessary because in this hour, there are many married believers praying to the Lord and asking Him to send them spouses. Additionally, there are many believers standing at the wedding altar about to marry someone who is already married, just as they, themselves are already married, only illegally.

The large number of believers and non-believers love music. The style of music we prefer is, of course, based on the content and intent of our hearts. This means that a secular man who loves the world and all it has to offer will love secular music. A man who's "straddling the fence" between the church and the world may love gospel hip hop or any other music that has the secular sounds and beats the world has come to love, all the while, playing gospel lyrics. This is because he is a person who has not fully separated himself from the world, nevertheless, he has no problem quoting scripture. Gospel hip hop is basically Christian words set to a worldly tone in a poetic way. Truth is, no one has ever witnessed a gospel hip hop artist usher in the presence of God and the reason is... God is not of this world; He is Spirit, therefore, those who worship Him must worship Him in Spirit and in Truth. Gospel hip hop, rap and any other worldly form of sharing the gospel is nothing more than soulish entertainment. Listeners are pulled into the sounds of the artist, since hip hop artists and rappers tend to have their own styles. Listeners also hear the lyrics, but of course, the artist's style, flow, stage presence, clothing and delivery are what most listeners pay attention to, because again, worldly gospel is not designed to usher God in. It's designed to entertain people who are still in a certain mindset, people who find it difficult to listen to or relate to traditional gospel or Christian music.

Romans 12:2: Do not be conformed to this world, but be transformed by the renewal of your mind, that by testing you may discern what is the will of God, what is good and acceptable and perfect.

Have you ever noticed how worldly some
church folks act when they see a secular artist
who's considered a celebrity? Some people
scream, some faint and others cry when in the
presence of certain celebrities. Why is this?
After all, a celebrity is nothing more than a
celebrated person, or a creature (creation of
God) who's been placed on a pedestal by the
world. People tend to react strongly around
their favorite celebrities because they have soul
ties with these people, and those soul ties were
established through the music. At the same
time, those soul ties are one-sided, meaning,
they are mentally soul tied to the artists they're
idolizing, but those artists are not soul tied to
them. Let's revisit the case of David and
Jonathan. Their bond was established early on
in their friendship and it was pretty much one-
sided. Remember, the Bible said Jonathan's soul
was knit to David's soul and he (Jonathan)
loved David as he loved himself. Again, what
this tells us is that soul ties can and are
oftentimes one-sided.

God told us to guard our hearts, and one of the

ways we guard our hearts is by ensuring that we don't allow the wrong people in our lives. The people we open our lives to will have access to our hearts, and because of this, they have the power to influence, better or ruin our lives. The greater the title we give to people, the more access we'll grant to them to our hearts. For example, whenever we refer to someone as our "best friend", we are pretty much saying that the person in question has access to our strengths, weaknesses, secrets, plans and innermost knowledge. It simply means we trust them with our lives. It means our hearts are not guarded from them. God told us to guard our hearts because every issue of life comes from there. When the wrong people have access to our hearts, they can sow discord, lies and seeds designed to lower our self-perception. For this reason, Satan is always sending people our way to pose as friends or people who can be trusted in our lives. They offer us advice, money, a place to stay, jobs and whatever else they can give us to gain access to our hearts. Of course, they don't know they're Satan-sent. They only know that there's something about us that intrigues them. Many of them successfully enter our lives, and before long, they begin to refer to themselves as our "best friends". This label not only requires that we lower our guards, but it also requires that we follow a set of unspoken rules, and these rules are their guidelines, or better yet, the terms of their friendship. For example, I'm sure you've met people who've gone on and on about the mistakes their past friends made. They then went on to tell you how they would have handled each situation and what a "real friend" would have done in that situation. What they're doing, in many cases, is passive-aggressively describing the terms of their friendship. They're teaching you what it means to be their friend and they're looking for your reaction to the stories they're telling you. They want to see if you'll fit well into their lives, or if nothing else, you can be easily molded and manipulated to fit into their lives. Now, this isn't to say that everyone who tells you stories about failed friendships is doing so because they're manipulative and have ulterior motives; after all, I tell my friends a few stories here and there. This is to say that many people do so because they're trying to gain access to our hearts, and again, God warns that we are to guard our hearts. With music, however, we don't guard our hearts unless the music is a style of music we find boring, offensive or strange. That's why Satan loves to use music to create soul ties with people.

Have you ever heard the expression, "I know that song by heart?" Of course, you have! When someone says they know a song by heart, they're really saying they've committed that song to memory. Unlike other pieces of information, music tends to be stored by our brains in our long-term memory banks. This is why we can recite the lyrics to songs years (or decades) after we've last heard them. We memorize music through a process of repetitious chanting, and that's why a songwriter will almost always include a verse in the song called the "hook". The hook makes the song memorable and usually summarizes what the song is about. Of course, not all songs have hooks but some of today's most popular styles of music involve hooks. Another way songwriters help listeners remember their songs is by writing songs with lyrics that rhyme. It is easier for a person to remember the next line of a song when it rhymes with the previous line. Lastly, one of the most popular ways to help listeners remember songs is through the use of beats. A beat is a series of sounds that are played together to create a rhythmic and repetitive tone. Like hooks, beats are a series of sounds that repeat themselves to encourage and promote the memory of a song. For example, you'll notice how children bop their heads when learning their alphabets. This rhythmic movement helps them to remember their alphabets. Additionally, people often bop their heads when listening to music. When listening to a song for the first time, people often move their heads to the beat to memorize the song, but in today's society, bopping the head is now looked upon as a listener's way of signaling that he or she approves or likes the music he or she is listening to.

There are many styles of music designed to entertain and mislead people, and almost everyone alive can find a style they're most interested in. The type of music we're most interested in is oftentimes a representation of the lifestyles we're living or the lives we desire to have. Of course, a song has enough power in it to influence another human being to desire a life different from the life he or she is living. For example, you'll notice that some rich kids end up hanging out in bad neighborhoods and listening to some of the most wicked forms of music, simply because the style of music they've grown to love tells them about a reality they cannot relate to. Now, this isn't to say that the music listened to in poverty stricken areas is always wicked, but you have to understand that in order for an artist to reach a group of people, he or she must make music the people can relate to.

If you were like myself, having grown up in poverty, you'll notice that a few people who were raised in poverty-stricken areas listened to styles of music that were different to the musical styles that most people in their communities listened to. Even though the majority of people who didn't personally know them weren't aware of the styles of music they listened to, they could always tell that they were different because they did not conform to the cultures most people in their areas had conformed to. In many cases, people were bullied, attacked or even killed simply because they stood out. One of the things that helped them to stand out the most, outside of their human-to-human relationships, was their preferred style of music because music oftentimes introduces the listener to a different culture, mindset or reality. At the same time, when a child does not fit in well to a community, that child is going to leave that community eventually, and that's why many people who have pretty much settled into certain lifestyles, mindsets and communities will oftentimes threaten or attack anyone who stands out. This doesn't just happen in poverty-stricken areas; this also happens in wealthy areas. A good example is a wealthy woman who gets tired of traveling the path her parents have carved out for her. Her parents desire that she goes to a certain school, surrounds herself with a certain class of people, marries a certain guy or a certain type of guy and lives a lifestyle that's not too different from their own. However, that woman wants to live an average life. She wants to be a nurse, marry an average guy, have a few children, and live in an area that's subpar to where she was raised. After aimlessly trying to get her to change her mind, her parents end up sending her to boarding school. When this doesn't work, they threaten to "cut her off" financially, meaning, they threaten to take away the financial inheritance they would have left her upon their deaths. Friends of the family, neighbors and many of the people in their social circles hear about her "rebellion", and forbid their children from communicating with her. Her peers mock her, and some even physically assault her. What's happening here is she's dared to stand out and people who've settled in mindsets don't fare too well around people who differ from themselves. That's the power music has over people.

Music is designed to reach the innermost parts of our souls. It influences so many aspects of our lives, but one of the most noticeable impacts music has on human beings is the impact music has on our emotions. You'll notice that one song could make or ruin your entire day. One song can make the difference between you getting married, remaining married or seeking a divorce. One song has the power to influence a person to fight, change their mind about something or even commit adultery. You see, unlike human-to-human friendships, an artist can influence a human being without having any personal contact with that person. At the same time, the artist is communicating with that person, and the more the listener tunes in to that artist, the less they'll guard their hearts against him/her. Before long, the listener is soul tied and the artist indirectly suggests to the listener how he or she should live, think, or reason. You'll notice that some people faint, perspire, lose their breath or scream frantically when in the presence of a highly celebrated artist, and this, of course, means they are likely soul tied to that artist. On the contrary though, the artist is not soul tied to them, meaning, they have no power to influence that artist's life or decisions. That's why people take to the media to express their opinions about the lives of the celebrities they've soul tied themselves to, especially when those celebrities' choices don't line up with their fairy-tale views of them. People don't like being influenced by individuals they have no influence over, so the media often serves as the vehicles average people use to be heard by the celebrities they've linked their souls (and finances) to. It's no different than romantically linking yourself to a human being, only to find yourself in a one-sided relationship. Since you've invested a lot into that relationship, you will expect a return on your investment, but when the person you love does not love you back, you will look for other ways to reach that person.

In addition to establishing soul ties between the listener and the artist, music also encourages people to establish soul ties with one another. Think about when you were a teenager, for example. Most of us have the same testimony. We were young and thought we were in love, so we would be on the phone in the wee hours of the night talking to our love interests. We would have soft music playing in the background and this music said everything we wanted to say and more. We began to identify certain songs as "our songs" with the people we were engaging with. Even if we never had sex with those people, we still identified certain songs as "our songs" and the reason for this was that those songs encouraged us to open our hearts. After a few conversations, we were soul tied to the people we so affectionately referred to as our boyfriends and girlfriends. Years later, many of us still remember our first, second, third and fourth lovers because we emotionally soul tied ourselves to them. Oftentimes, certain songs will bring those exes into our remembrance because we have reserved those songs in our hearts as "our songs" with them.

Music encourages emotional soul ties, but emotional soul ties almost always lead to sexual soul ties. Music helps with relationships by saying to both parties what the other person is feeling, or by saying what the other person wants to hear, even though it is a lie. For example, let's say Jacob is dating Christina. Christina has opened her heart to Jacob and is falling deeply in love with him, which, in truth, means she's being bewitched. *To be romantically bewitched is to be lied to or to lie to one's self for the sake of moving forward in a relationship that shouldn't have ever started.*

Jacob, on the other hand, does not feel the same way about Christina as she feels about him. However, Jacob is sexually attracted to Christina, but he knows that Christina won't have sex with him unless he allows her to establish an emotional soul tie with him. Jacob is a man of very few words and he's not comfortable displaying affection or speaking poetically to anyone, so anytime Jacob calls Christina, he plays soft music in the background. He chooses songs that say what he knows Christina wants to hear, and he spends a lot of time being silent while he's on the phone with Christina. He does this because he wants her to hear the sweet melodies and lyrics of the songs playing in the background. Christina gets lost in the music, listening to the artist who's helping her to bewitch herself. She loses herself in her imaginations, not understanding that Jacob is simply trying to get her to stop guarding her heart. You see, when she stops guarding her heart, she'll stop guarding her body, and he knows this. Before long, Jacob has arranged to be alone with Christina and he is sure to bring a CD of the songs he believes lowers her guards the most. After Christina has emotionally soul tied herself to Jacob, she freely offers her body to him, hoping that everything the artists said through their music is truly how Jacob feels about her. After having sex with Christina a few times, Jacob stops calling Christina and she realizes that she's been duped. Jacob used music to get what he wanted from Christina because Jacob realized the power of spoken words, even words he didn't have to speak them.

God wants us to guard our hearts. As a matter

of fact, He commanded that we guard our hearts. Any music you listen to is going to influence and affect your life, and you will establish soul ties with the artists you listen to the most. Now, some soul ties are godly; for example, if you begin to love and pray for an artist who encourages you to follow the Lord through their song ministry. Then again, some soul ties are ungodly; for example, if you begin to reverence and love an artist who encourages you to give in to the desires of your flesh. If you end up listening to music that encourages you to go against the Lord, you will become full of beliefs and thoughts that will challenge your relationship with God. Sure, the soul likes music that entertains the flesh, but we can't be led by our flesh. The Bible tells us to be led by the Spirit. If you want your life to prosper, you need to avoid feeding junk food (music that does not align with the Word of God) to your soul. Keep blessing yourself by feeding your mind, body, spirit and soul the Word of God. Gospel and Christian music encourages, uplifts and ministers to the spirit of a man, but secular music entertains the flesh. Of course, there are some secular songs posing as gospel and Christian songs, just as there are some secular artists posing as gospel and Christian artists. Nevertheless, it's pretty easy to distinguish between true gospel or Christian music versus secular by simply paying attention to whichever part of you it appeals to. For example, I met a woman who was newly saved and she said to me that whenever she heard certain gospel songs or artists, she felt like dancing the same way she danced when she was in the clubs. I explained to her that she was listening to music that appealed to the flesh, and therefore, wasn't truly gospel music; it was simply music designed to entertain. Anytime we listen to music designed to minister to us, our spirits will begin to respond and we may weep, praise God or simply be encouraged. But, anytime we listen to secular music posing as gospel music, our flesh will respond, and even though some gospel and Christian songs make us want to dance, secular gospel tones will make us want to dance like the world. If you find yourself praise dancing, it's probably because your spirit is being fed and ministered to, but if you find yourself breaking out those old dance moves you used to show off in the club, your flesh is being entertained.

Be careful who you open your heart to. Ask the Lord to lead you in all your ways, even when it comes to the music you listen to. If the music isn't adding to your life, you'd better believe it's taking away from your life.

Musical soul ties are real, and again, they help us establish emotional links between ourselves and others, but when those soul ties are not God-approved, they are ungodly. Ungodly soul ties only set us up for ungodly results.

Am I Soul Tied to Anyone?

I've come across many men and women who question whether God has someone specifically for them or not. They've practiced abstinence and waited patiently (and impatiently) for their God-appointed spouses for years. They've helped some, mentored others and did what they believed to be their Christian duties. Time and time again, they've watched with green eyes as their not-so-faithful friends, family members and co-workers announced their wedding engagements. Because of this, many of them began to question their personal beliefs and convictions. They told themselves that maybe... just maybe... they are responsible for finding their own mates. Maybe... just maybe... they weren't supposed to be waiting; they were supposed to be pursuing. Because of this, many of them have begun to position themselves to find or be found by anyone who has a mutual romantic interest in them. When they've come across such souls, they've entered relationships with them, even though they saw that the people they were linking themselves to needed to be patched up in a few places. Before long, they were standing at the courthouse or at a local church and exchanging vows with the people they've chosen for themselves. With tears of joy in their eyes, they've basked in the spotlights that were their weddings, hoping their sins have paid off for them; after all, sin requires a sacrifice and they've sacrificed the will of God to get what they wanted. One to five years later, they are tearfully signing their names on the divorce papers their estranged spouses have sent them. Their signatures represent so many things, even though they may be oblivious to them. Their signatures confirmed:

1. The Word of God is true, and therefore, cannot be overridden. "For the word of the LORD is right; and all his works are done in truth" (Psalms 33:4 KJV).
2. They rose up against the Word and lost. "But if it is from God, you will not be able to overthrow them. You may even

find yourselves fighting against God!"
(Acts 5:39 NLT).

3. God is love, and love cannot fail,
   meaning, their marriages did not have
   God in them, therefore, their marriages
   were loveless or godless marriages and
   that's why they failed. "Anyone who does
   not love does not know God, because
   God is love (1 John 4:8).

4. You can't trust yourself; only God is
   trustworthy. "The heart is deceitful
   above all things, and desperately
   wicked: who can know it?" (Jeremiah
   17:9 KJV).

5. One popular adage says: If you want to
   make God laugh, tell Him what your
   plans are. "Many are the plans in a
   person's heart, but it is the Lord's
   purpose that prevails" (Proverbs 19:21
   NIV).

Many have come to realize that there is NO
way around God's Word. It's normal to want to
move things along in your life a lot faster than
the speed they're going in, but every step of

our lives, every breath we take, and every decision we make is designed to get us to where we're called to be... even if we're taking a few steps backwards. Anytime we're being held up or held back, it's because we have not accepted the truth about something, and God won't bless us if we're full of lies. For example, in the few years I've been in ministry, I've counseled a lot of women, and quite a few of them have been victims of what I like to call the "bait to wait" maneuver. What happened was that they were romantically linked (soul tied) to some guys who they were convinced they would end up marrying someday. Some of them had even married the guys. At some point in their relationships, things took a dark turn and the guys left, but not before placing the entire blame of the breakup on those women. They convinced the women that something they said or did was the reason behind their breakups, and then, they pretended to be incurably affected by their partners' ways. They pretended that they had been planning to marry those women before they offended them and "caused" them to end the relationship altogether. They then went on to enter new relationships (almost immediately after the breakup), and the women who were left behind were left believing that they ruined the best thing that had ever happened to them. Because of this, those women don't know how to truly move on. They kept the doors of their hearts open for their new exes because they wanted to right their wrongs. They didn't realize that the guys they soul tied themselves to had simply entered new relationships and didn't want to cut them out of their lives entirely because they were self-centered. They knew the women they were leaving behind were good women, but they also knew that those women would never willfully allow them to court other women. They wanted to see if their new relationships would be better than their current relationships, so they provoked their lovers, knowing full well that those women would speak their minds. They then pretended to be overwhelmingly hurt by their current lovers' choice of words (or actions) and they used those words (or actions) to justify ending the relationships. To ensure their new exes would not move on with their lives, they pretended to be the victims of their current lovers' foul tempers or not-so-wise choices. After their exes accepted the full blame, they were able to walk away with their exes on hold. These exes will oftentimes enter new relationships, but they'll keep the door of their hearts open for the ones they believed they wrongfully mishandled. They were victims of the "bait to wait" maneuver where a guy finds an excuse to abandon one woman so he could romantically entertain another woman or other women. Such a guy wants the ability to come back to the woman he's walked away from if his new relationship does not work out the way he hopes it will. At the same time, should he come back, he doesn't want to be the one responsible for ending the relationship the first time, because in his mind, this gives the woman too much power. He wants to come back and change the terms of the relationship to his own advantage.

A lot of women and men in the church today have been victims of the "bait to wait" maneuver, and even though they keep praying and asking God to send them their God-appointed spouses, they wait in vain because they're still soul tied to their former lovers. They don't realize it, but their souls are on hold while the people they're soul tied to are on the other line entertaining other people. Many of these women and men remain abstinent while waiting for their God-appointed spouses, but they wait in vain because they are not free to marry.

How do you know if you're soul tied to someone? Below are 18 clues that you may be soul tied to someone else. Please note that if you find yourself on this list, the best way to respond is to talk to the Lord and let Him reveal the condition of your heart. All too often, people stay bound because they stay in denial, but when you are serious about moving forward in the Lord, you will take every necessary step you need to take to get and remain free. Always remember that challenging the truth won't change it.

18 Signs You're Still Soul Tied to an Ex

1. **You still feel guilty about a past breakup, and if given the chance, you'd reconcile with your former lover-** Again, many men and women use the "bait to wait" maneuver to keep their former lovers from moving on with their lives. If you still have unanswered questions or feel you need closure, you're still soul tied.

2. **You're still hanging out with your ex's family-** I've come across this more times than I care to admit... especially with women. All too often, a soul tied person will stay close to the family of the person they're soul tied to, and then, they will attempt to justify their relationship with their ex's family. Many say things like, "The family didn't do anything to me, so why should I cut them off?!" or "I knew the family before I knew him or her!" The truth is... they are still soul tied to their former lovers and wanting to maintain a front row seat in their exes' lives. They also want to be the

"first draft pick" of the family. When a person is truly ready to move forward and has accepted that the relationship was never meant to be, they'll make the necessary sacrifices, and that includes, severing all ties to the family unless children are involved.

3. **You're still hanging around your ex's friends-** Again, a lot of people justify hanging on to the familiar when they're still bound by soul ties. A soul tied person will oftentimes remain friends with the friends of their exes or anyone tied to the friends of their exes. Again, the reason for this is they want to gain or retain favor with the people who are connected with their exes. At the same time, they want to receive up-to-the-minute updates about their exes' lives.

4. **You still get butterflies in your stomach anytime you spot one of your exes-** Your body will always tell you how your soul feels. Remember, the soul consists of the mind, will and emotions. That queasiness or

nervousness you feel when your ex comes around is your mind and emotions telling you that you are still tied to that person.

5. **If you run into one of your exes, you worry about how you look-** Truthfully, many will say that they simply want to look good in front of their exes, even though they don't want them back, but please know this: You can be soul tied to someone and still not want to reconcile with them. This confusing truth is the reason so many people don't seek to be set free from ungodly soul ties. After all, they don't realize they're bound. If one or more of your exes still possess the power to move you or change the direction of your thinking, you are still soul tied to them.

6. **You have trust issues-** Trust issues are oftentimes the result of unforgiveness and a lack of knowledge. When you are truly set free from ungodly soul ties, one of the gifts God hands you is understanding, and then, when you

understand why the relationship didn't work out, He teaches you to embrace accountability. When you accept your part in the startup and breakup of that ungodly relationship, it's easier to forgive the ex. When you forgive the ex, your trust will automatically begin to rebuild itself.

7. **You're having a lot of dreams about a particular ex of yours-** The heart will oftentimes tell the mind when it's bound. Dreams are like smoke signals, whereas, the heart responds to its current condition by alerting the conscious mind about what's hiding in the subconscious mind. Now, dreams don't always mean you're soul tied to someone. Sometimes, the enemy will give you dreams just to confuse and bind you, but the difference is when you're soul tied, the dreams are frequent, and they'll oftentimes move you to believe that your ex is the right person for you.

8. **No one can seem to measure up to**

one of your exes- Do you find yourself comparing each and every one of your romantic interests to a particular ex of yours? If so, you're still soul tied to that ex. The reason for this is you don't have the understanding you'll need to seek freedom from that soul tie. Some people ask to be free from ungodly soul ties with their mouths, but in their hearts, they desire to remain linked to certain people because they aren't truly convinced that those people are not right for them.

9. **You keep checking your ex's social media pages online-** This is one of the most common and telltale side effects of an unsevered, ungodly soul tie. The reason people check their exes' social media pages is because social media involves live interaction and people tend to update their social media pages quite often. When you're still soul tied to someone, you want to be a part of their present lives, just as you were a part of their pasts. Social media affords people

the ability to stay abreast of their former lovers' lives and relationship statuses.

10. **You compare yourself to one or more of your exes' current love interests-** This one really needs no explanation. When you compare yourself to one or more of your ex's current lovers, it simply means you are mentally competing with them. A competition always involves a winner and a loser, and no one competes to lose unless the game is fixed. Again, this does not mean you want the ex back; it simply means your ex is still a part of your heart, and therefore, a part of your choices. Anyone who can affect your choices has too much power in your life.

11. **You're angry with one or more of your exes' current love interests-** Again, this doesn't require much of an explanation. One of the things we see commonly is how a relationship where children are involved can get pretty messy. The woman may still be soul tied to the father of her child or children, and

because of this, she will dislike or even hate the woman her ex is currently with. This happens with men as well, but whenever a man or woman has unjustifiable anger toward their exes' lovers, they are still soul tied to those exes. Of course, every person who dislikes their ex's current love interests will find reasons to justify their dislike, but the truth is... when the soul is tied to another person, the flesh arises to compete.

12. **You intentionally go to events you know your ex will likely come to-** It's Friday night and your old High School is hosting its Homecoming dance. Your ex happens to have a son who goes to your old High School, and you know your ex goes to every one of his son's events, so you look for an excuse to show up at the dance. You are undoubtedly still soul tied to that ex! When the soul is no longer bound to another soul, the person in question is demoted in the heart. They will transition from being

important individuals with the power to influence your thoughts and decisions to being nothing more than familiar faces that can easily get lost in a crowd. How important someone is to you will always tell you whether you are free from them or still soul tied to them.

13. **Some or most of your plans for success evolve around making the ex regret the day he or she left you-** The ex should not be a part of your conscious mind or your decision-making. The average believer is bound by one or more of their exes, and because of this, they've centered their lives around their exes. Many of their decisions, if not all of them, are centered around making their exes jealous or regretful, and this means they still have their exes in their hearts and on their minds! Think of it this way. If you are married to someone, you intend to live with that person, right? When searching for your new house, your spouse would be a part of the decision-making

process, and you will buy a home that both of you agree upon. The same goes for someone you're soul tied to. Even though they don't come with you in body, you will always take them with you in your heart. You will buy homes, cars and items you know your ex would love to have because you want to make the ex jealous. You will do many of the things you know your ex has always wanted to do because you want your ex's attention. What you're doing is creating the perfect setting for your ex, and then, denying him or her entry into your new setup. This means you will forfeit your dreams and the dreams of your spouse just to get revenge on your ex. Of course, this means you're still soul tied to that person, and that's why he or she is still living in your mind and heart today, and that's why your ex is still a part of the decision-making process.

14. **A particular song or smell still brings the ex to your remembrance-** When we were young, most of us would lie

down on our beds and talk to our boyfriends or girlfriends while listening to the sounds of sensual music. We would let the music bewitch us into believing that the person on the other line was the guy or girl of our dreams. We would then declare a song to be our special song, and every time we heard it, we would think of our boyfriends or girlfriends. Additionally, whenever they came around, we became even more intoxicated by the smells of their cologne or perfume. Then, that inevitable doomsday came and we broke up, but for some reason, we managed to hold a seat in our hearts for our exes. You see, we could override those memories with new memories, but we oftentimes choose not to do so because we love to revisit those memories. For example, it is easy to take a song and create new memories with that song, or to take a scent and create new memories with that scent. Nevertheless, we choose to reserve seats for our exes, and this causes so many people to remain soul tied to their exes twenty and thirty years after they've broken up!

15. **You're still waiting for your ex to "get back" what he or she has done to you-** Again, unforgiveness means you're still soul tied to the ex. A lot of people try to use the Bible to justify wishing evil upon their exes, and this is blatantly wicked! If the ex is a part of your subconscious mind, he or she is a part of your heart. If your ex is a part of your heart, he or she will influence the direction of your life. "Guard your heart above all else, for it determines the course of your life" (Proverbs 4:23).

16. **You directly or indirectly encourage your children to be mad at their father, mother, or one of their parents' current lovers-** Soul tied people sometimes want their children to harbor the same ill feelings toward their estranged parents as they do. Additionally, they want their children to

reject their father or mothers' current love interests because they feel their spots are being taken. Of course, this is done by an incredibly selfish, immature and inconsiderate parent. Sadly enough, this is rather common in the twenty first century.

17. **You're holding on to old trinkets and gifts that were given to you by the ex-** Soul tied people tend to keep memoirs and souvenirs of their past experiences, especially their experiences with the people they've soul tied themselves to. These trinkets include, but are not limited to: notes, pictures, jewelry, clothing, etc. This is because they want to mentally revisit those old relationships from time to time. Of course, this means they are still soul tied to their exes.

18. **Every time you run into one of your exes, you talk about your failed relationship with him or her-** Where there is no closure, there are soul ties! When you're truly free from someone,

you won't desire to talk with them about the past because there is no future for the two of you. People who are still soul tied think they need closure, when in truth, they need to be delivered from those ungodly soul ties.

Of course, there are many more symptoms of intact ungodly soul ties, but we must always remain prayerful and pay attention to our own hearts and motives. We have to be brutally honest with ourselves; that way, we will immediately seek to be set free from any ungodly mindsets and bondage we find ourselves in. Are you still soul tied to anyone? That's a question only you and the Lord can truly answer. If you are still soul tied with someone, you've seen the signs that you are. The question is... Will you be honest with yourself and seek to be freed from every ungodly soul tie that has you bound?

Taking Your Freedom Back

Being bound by ungodly soul ties can be pretty taxing. As a matter of fact, a person bound by ungodly soul ties is a person who will unknowingly limit God from moving freely throughout his or her life. That's because ungodly soul ties imprison any and everyone who is bound by them. A prisoner can't enjoy an inheritance until he or she has been set free. A prisoner can't venture outside the walls of the prison he or she is in, and a prisoner is considered the property of the institution that's holding him or her captive. For this reason, if you want to receive and enjoy every blessing God has for you, you need to make sure that you are not a bondman or bondwoman to ungodly soul ties or any other type of sin.

At this very moment, there are many people in the world who are bound by ungodly soul ties, and many of them don't realize they're bound. The enemy has managed to convince many that soul ties don't exist, even though there is biblical proof that they do. Some people think soul ties only exist between a man and his wife the moment they get married, not understanding that marriage, in God's eyes, isn't established when we say, "I do". Marriage is established through sexual contact. Nevertheless, soul ties are real, and the sad reality is many people are bound by them today.

How can one be set free from ungodly soul ties? Below are 25 pointers to help you free yourself from the enemy's grasp:

1. **Repent of the deed that got you bound in the first place-** People don't realize how important repentance is to God. That's because the average person thinks to repent means to apologize, and for this reason, many people find themselves repeating the same sins they apologized for. To repent means to turn your heart and mind back to God. It means to be regretful of the wrongs you've done, and then, demonstrate

your changed mind by not repeating the sin. If ungodly associations were the tools the enemy used to bind you, repent of those ungodly associations and be careful who you befriend in the future. If sexual immorality was the tool the enemy used to bind you, repent of your fornication, end the relationship with the person you fornicated with, and commit to never fornicating again.

2. **Forgive everyone who has ever hurt, betrayed or wronged you in any type of way-** As we discussed earlier, unforgiveness makes it impossible for a person to be set free from ungodly soul ties. The reason for this is that soul ties affect our minds, will and emotions, just as unforgiveness affects our minds, will and emotions. Having a soul tie severed is similar to having a chain broken between the hearts of two people, but being in unforgiveness is similar to chaining a person to your heart until you think they've served their time or paid the price for whatever wrongs

they've done to you. Why would God
break the soul tie if you're still trying to
bind that person with unforgiveness?

3. **Forgive yourself-** Some people remain
   bound to ungodly soul ties because of
   guilt. Maybe they were responsible for
   the ending of their relationships, or
   maybe they were made to feel
   responsible for the ending of their
   relationships. It doesn't matter why or
   how you became unforgiving, the truth
   is... you can't move on until you free
   yourself. Please understand that no one
   is perfect and we all make mistakes.
   Some people make small mistakes and
   pay great prices, whereas, others make
   huge mistakes and pay small prices. It's
   never a wise move to get caught up in
   what's fair or unfair. What you have to
   do is make a <u>conscious</u> effort to forgive
   yourself for every wrong you've done;
   after all, whenever you truly repented to
   God, He forgave you. Now ask Him to
   help you forgive yourself. You will never
   truly let go of a person or be free from

that person if you keep reliving the past.

4. **Beware of the same spirits in different people-** It is human nature to be drawn to what's familiar and Satan knows this, so he likes to encourage us to bind ourselves to "types" of people. For example, a woman who has soul tied herself to a tall, take-charge kind of guy will oftentimes find herself in relationships with tall, take-charge kind of guys. A man who tends to be attracted to seductive, feisty women will oftentimes look past women who radiate holiness and submission and go after just about any Jezebel or Delilah he sees. Please know that your soul is familiar with a certain type of person and spirit. Familiar spirits have the power to do the most damage because we don't question people who are bound by the spirits we are familiar with. That's why people tend to date the same spirit in different people. Ask the Lord to sever all ungodly soul ties and familiar associations. Bind every unclean spirit

that is hindering, attacking, seducing or preying on you in Jesus name. You have the power to tell those spirits where to go and how long they'll be there. Send them into the abyss until the day of Judgment in Jesus name!

5. **Disassociate yourself from anyone who links you to your ex (except the children)-** This includes your ex's family, friends, co-workers and the like. Now, I do understand that I'll get a lot of backlash behind this one because some people have been exceptionally nice to us, and we don't want to sever all ties with them just because our exes made foolish choices. Nevertheless, we have to pray about EVERY relationship we have with people and ask the Lord if those relationships are good in His sight. You'll find that in dealings with people affiliated with your ex, God will more than likely command you to sever all ties. This doesn't mean the people were bad to you; it simply means that God has something or someone better for

you, and He is not going to send one of His favored children into a complicated and uncomfortable situation. If God tells you to stay connected, that's great, but ask Him to make and maintain the connection so that it does not take an ungodly turn.

6. **Disassociate yourself from ungodly friends, family members and anyone who's bound-** Bound people bind people, and how can two walk together except they be in agreement? Our casual associations will always set us up for other soul ties, and that's why it's important that we not be bound to anyone through ungodly soul ties.

7. **Fill yourself with the Word of God-** The more Word you have in your heart, the less room you'll have for foolishness. The Word of God will heal every broken place in your heart. It will fill every void in your life and restore what's been stolen from you. You can't fully recover without the Word, so make sure you read the Word of God daily... several

times a day if you can!

8. **Don't meditate on the wrong thoughts or dreams-** I've counseled many people who were bound by soul ties, and one thing they all seem to have in common is the plaguing thoughts and dreams they have about their exes. People know their exes aren't right for them, but they will still lie down and meditate on a dream they had, a memory that surfaced or something that was said, and this makes being free from that ungodly soul tie next to impossible. Remember to cast down all imaginations and every high thing that exalts itself against the knowledge (Word) of God and bring into captivity every thought to the obedience of Christ (the Word). In other words, call those imaginations lies and speak the Word over your mind. When on the battleground, you don't look at the enemy's plans and consider them; you simply remind that ole devil that he's already defeated.

9. **Tell yourself the truth... your ex was not "the one"**- Another binding thought is the belief that the ex was possibly the one for you. Most people have that one ex they thought they would spend their lives with, and even after they've been broken up from those exes for years, they still have trouble believing that those exes were not the ones. Be honest with yourself and stop trying to find ways to make your ex fit into your future. Ask the Lord to show you the undeniable truth so that you can move on.

10. **Take accountability for your own actions**- One of the easiest ways to stay bound is to project all the blame onto the ex. Take accountability for your own wrongs, even if your wrong was simply getting with that ex in the first place. For example, I married two unsaved men when I was young in the faith, and even though they'd done some pretty despicable things to me, I was able to forgive them by accepting the fact that

I'd wronged them just as much as they'd wronged me. How so? Both times, I knew the Word of God said to not be unequally yoked with unbelievers, but I thought I could make believers out of them, so it was wrong of me to take people who were content with their lives, and then, try to lure them into the church. True ministry doesn't happen by force or coercion; a person is simply invited to Christ, and they have the freedom to accept or reject that invitation.

11. **Don't bind yourself to any form of debt-** I know that this may make absolutely no sense to you, but the truth is... debt is a form of bondage. Anytime a person places themselves in debt, they familiarize themselves with bondage. The greater the bondage you're in, the more likely you are to bind yourself to an individual you think can help you to free yourself. For example, a woman who goes out and gets a lot of credit cards won't have any reservations about

getting with a guy she feels can get her out of her debt. She'll even have trouble letting go of the men she feels helped her the most. Quite the contrary, a woman who is a good steward over her finances won't need a man to bail her out, and because of this, she is more likely to seek to be freed and remain free from ungodly soul ties than a woman who is bound by debt.

12. **Throw away any and everything your ex gave you (except the children)-** Remember, the battlefield is in the mind and the enemy wants to take you back to familiar grounds so he can bind you time after time. If you go to God and ask Him to free you from all ungodly soul ties, one thing you'll notice is that He will bring your attention to something or some things your ex has given you. Those trinkets are point of contacts which allow your ex to still have a place in your heart and home, and therefore, they serve as tools for the enemy to keep you bound. Don't give those items

to your children or someone close to you. Instead, the best thing to do is to throw them away.

13. **Throw away any furniture you've had sex with your ex on-** Anything you've given yourself on has become an altar because you presented yourself as a living sacrifice. With sex, blood or blood cells are always shed, and therefore, your ex has left a part of himself or herself any and everywhere the two of you have had sex. You need to move every aspect of your ex out of your life to be wholly set free, and again, this does not include the children.

14. **Throw away all undergarments you wore while actively engaging in fornication with your ex-** Please see number 13. A woman reached out to me some years ago. She was upset because she'd woken up that day and found herself burning with desire. She tried to overlook how she felt, but she finally gave in to those ungodly desires and masturbated. She called me up, feeling

regretful about what she'd done, and the first thing the Lord laid on my heart was to tell her how the garments we've worn in sin affect us and why we should throw them all away. Surprised, she then told me that she hadn't washed clothes in a while, and because of this, she didn't have any clean undergarments, so she found an old pair of underwear she'd worn when she was a stripper. She'd just put them on the night before (for the first time in years), and the next morning, she woke up burning with desire. Please understand that witches use material things as point of contacts to perform their witchcraft. If a witch will use material things as point of contacts to perform their sorcery, Satan (the father of all witches) also uses material things as point of contacts.

15. **Change your mind about certain songs and scents-** First and foremost, you should not be listening to any ungodly music, so I definitely don't want to encourage you to go back and listen

to anything that rises against the Word of God. As a matter of fact, you shouldn't listen to anything that goes against the Word of God. Nevertheless, there may be some good and Godly songs that remind you of your ex, just as there may be some scents that remind you of your ex. Take those songs and scents from that ex. How do you do this? By simply listening to those songs and creating new memories with them. *Make sure those new memories aren't tied to new romantic interests.* A song can remind you of the times you walked alone on a beach or when you used to hang out at a park. Additionally, buy those cologne scents or perfumes for your loved ones so that you can associate those scents with someone else and not the ex.

16. **If you can, avoid going to places your ex frequents-** How far are you willing to go to get and remain free? If you know your ex frequents a park in your area, try to avoid that park. Some would argue

that they don't want to limit themselves because of their exes, but that line of reasoning is why so many of those same people are bound to someone through ungodly soul ties. You can resume going to places like the local park, restaurants and the like once that soul tie is completely severed, but when you're seeking to be set free, you need to avoid your ex at all costs. Additionally, check your motives behind wanting to hang out or visit some of the places your exes frequent. Some people tell themselves and others that they simply like going to those places, but the truth is... they want to see or be seen by their exes. We can and do lie to ourselves sometimes, but the way to try yourself is by paying attention to your motives. If you like to visit a local park and your ex happens to like to visit that same park, are you hoping to see the ex anytime you go there? What happens when you don't see your ex? Do you leave early or become discouraged? Do you go out of your way to ensure you look your best anytime you visit that park? What type of thoughts do you have when you're preparing to go to the park and while on your way there? The answers to these questions will tell you your motives.

17. **End all communications with the ex if you don't have children with him or her-** When you first break up with someone, you're still soul tied to that person; that is, until you ask the Lord to set you free. Even if you ask God to set you free immediately after the breakup, you will find that God won't always immediately free you. Instead, He will take you through a process designed to keep you from returning to the sin that led you to your ex in the first place. God is strategic in His doings, so when you are in the process of being set free, you should never continue associating with the people you are being set free from. This only makes the process more difficult, more lengthy and more painful. At the same time, once you are set free,

you should never communicate with the people God has set you free from unless God establishes a connection with the two of you. The reason is we can be set free of soul ties established through sex, and end up reentering emotional soul ties with the people we were once sexually bound to. Of course, these emotional soul ties will lead to more illegal sex, unforgiveness or having our lives be hindered because of the bondage we've reentered. Your ex is an ex for a reason. You don't need to constantly remind yourself of why they are your exes; you simply need to be free and remain free.

18. **If you do have children with your ex, keep all communications about the children-** It's a good idea to be friendly with the ex. It's even a good idea to consider yourself friends for the sake of the children, but be very careful that you don't cross those blurred boundaries and end up emotionally soul tied to your ex. Of course, the large majority of

parents are still soul tied to the fathers
and mothers of their children, and for
the ones who have been set free, there
is always a risk of them reentering
emotional soul ties with their exes since
they have to repeatedly deal with them
for the sake of their children. Boundaries
have to be set to ensure you don't end
up emotionally soul tied to the father or
mother of your children. For example,
it's not a good idea to share the details
of your personal life with your ex unless
it directly or indirectly affects your
children. If you are emotionally soul tied
to your ex, that soul tie will affect every
romantic relationship you attempt to
have.

19. **Recognize the players in the soul tie
    game-** Satan is going to send people to
    keep you bound or to bind you again;
    that's without a question. For example,
    you'll notice that some of your friends
    will always tell you whenever they run
    into one of your exes. They'll also tell
    you who that ex was with, what your ex's

new love interest looks like, and how your ex responded to seeing them. Make no mistake about it... these people are not your friends. They are friendly enemies. No true friend will want to see you still groveling over an ex. Additionally, there will likely be some family members, church members, co-workers and complete strangers who'll stop you from time-to-time just to tell you about the latest news that is your ex's life. Stop them! Always stop people from flooding your ear gates with news about your ex.

20. **Give yourself the necessary time to heal-** I remember when I was going through my second divorce. It was early in the breakup and my heart was still aching behind the breakup, nevertheless, I was more than determined to resume my daily activities. I kept trying to distract myself by working harder and longer, but the Lord eventually dealt with me and allowed me to see that I had begun

operating as a broken vessel. Of course, I had to take some time to myself to pray and properly heal so I could truly move on with my life. The same goes for you. All too often, we want to fast forward past the pain and go back to living life as usual, but the reality is those soul ties still need to be broken. Some people learn to live without their exes, and some people are sincerely grateful that their relationships with their exes did not last, nevertheless, they are still soul tied to those people. The average person thinks that because they are over another human being or have adjusted to life without that person that they are no longer soul tied to them, but this is not true. Only God can sever a soul tie, and if we haven't asked Him to sever all ungodly soul ties and divorce us from every person we've married through our sins, we are still linked to those people.

21. **Uproot the old imaginations and replace them with new ones-** We tend

to make plans for our lives with the people we romantically link ourselves to, and whenever we break up with those people, those plans will oftentimes still remain. It's not uncommon to hear someone say they'd plan to buy a huge home in a certain neighborhood with their ex, and they have no intentions of giving up that plan. The truth is... to be free of ungodly soul ties, we have to allow God to clean our mental slates and give us new plans. Sometimes, similar or even better plans will arise, and we'll be able to live out those plans with the people God has appointed for our lives, but we can never get to a new place holding on to old things. Start some new imaginations, but this time, don't put a face on the person you will share your life with if you aren't already married. Just make plans to do the things you have always wanted to do by yourself and with your God-ordained spouse someday.

22. **Make a conscious effort to stay off**

your ex's (or anyone associated with your ex) social media pages- So, you just heard that your ex is getting married and you want to confirm or deny the news by going to your ex's Facebook page. This behavior is common for you because you're still connected to the people who are connected to your ex, and they make sure that you are informed about the latest events in your ex's life. You go onto the ex's page and see your ex sharing engagement pictures. You smile, and then, boldly proclaim that the marriage won't work because of the ex's ways. What you're doing is treating your ex's profile like a crystal ball, and whenever you see your ex happy, you begin to speak word curses over his or her life. This is witchcraft, believe it or not. That's why you have to forgive, and that's why it's important for you to distance yourself from the ex in every way possible. If you have to block the ex to stop yourself from visiting his/her profile, then do so.

23. **Tell yourself the truth and nothing but the truth-** A lot of people remain soul tied because they keep lying to themselves about how they really feel. How many times have you come across a man who's boasted on not caring about his ex or anything she does, but whenever he sees his ex out somewhere, he stops and questions her about her life? The problem is... he's not being truthful with himself. He's learned to live without the ex, and he's learned to speak the language of a person who has been made whole, but in truth, he's still soul tied, broken and confused. Tell yourself the truth. If you're not over one or more of your exes, be honest with yourself so you can be set free. Lying to yourself won't make the soul tie go away; it will simply delay your deliverance.

24. **Do something new in your life... often-** Sometimes, our lives are nothing more than a series of routines we've

mastered, and anytime we live monotonous lives, it'll be easy for us to find ourselves bound by soul ties. Why is this? Because a new relationship represents something new happening in our lives, and we can and will put more of ourselves into those relationships than someone who lives a more eventful life. Dare to do something new. Dare to get past a fear of yours. Dare to dream again. For example, if you've never traveled to another country, make plans to do so. If you've never thought about learning a new language, consider doing so. If you can't swim and want to learn how to swim, take swimming classes. Our old plans often involve our exes, but when we dare to make new plans for our lives, plans that we ordinarily wouldn't have made, we open our hearts to new realms of possibilities, and this makes it easier for us to be set free from ungodly soul ties. How so? Let's say that a man named Heath is soul tied to a woman named Catherine. Heath and Catherine have been broken up for years, but they are still soul tied to one another. Heath and Catherine's relationship goals were to get married, have three children, settle down in New York and vacation out of the country once a year. Heath is a dental hygienist and Catherine is a school teacher. Heath has never thought of any other life other than the one he'd planned with Catherine, and now, Heath is being plagued with thoughts of Catherine. What should he do? Heath should be daring and revise his plans. Heath could consider going back to school to become a dentist. Heath could consider starting his own dental practice. Heath could consider living in another state. Heath could consider traveling the world more. Heath could consider not planning the amount of children he will have. Instead, Heath can simply decide to let God decide how many children he and his future wife will have. Being daring and venturing outside the comforts of our old plans makes it easier for us to open ourselves to God and ask Him to deliver us from the people who are not a part His plans for us.

25. **Ask the Lord to sever all ungodly soul ties from your life-** God said, "You have not because you ask not (see James 4:2)". No man can separate a soul tie. We need God to do this for us, but at the same time, we have to understand that when God delivers us from ungodly soul ties, He oftentimes takes us through a process designed to help us remain free. For example, let's say that you are the parent of an eighteen year old boy. It's summer time and your son has gotten a job at a restaurant downtown. He asks you if he can drive one of your cars to work and you agree. After all, he has his driver's license and you feel comfortable with him driving. One day, you get a call from him stating that he backed into a car while trying to parallel park. You race to the scene and exchange insurance information with the owner of the

vehicle your son has hit. Your son is very apologetic and you know he didn't hit the car with malicious intent; it was truly an accident, so you're not angry with him. This doesn't change the fact that there will be consequences, however. The next day, your son comes to ask if he can use your car again, and you tell him "no." You explain to your son that you are going to put him in some driving classes so he can learn to parallel park. You're not withholding the car from your son to punish him. You are simply saying he needs to go through a process of learning to parallel park before you are comfortable letting him drive your car again. That's how God works. Sometimes, we have to go through processes, and even though we are sorrowful and repentant of the deeds we've done, we still have to be taught better so we can do better. Again, ask the Lord to deliver you from all ungodly soul ties, but be prepared for the process you're about to endure as well. This process is going to help develop, nurture and mature you. This process is absolutely necessary for your growth, deliverance and success.

Please know that if anyone wants to be delivered from ungodly soul ties, God will deliver them if they ask Him. However, seeking to be free means you have to want to remain free. Some people want to be freed from ungodly soul ties with certain people, but they have no problem joining themselves to others through ungodly soul ties. In situations like this, they aren't truly repentant, and therefore, they haven't approached God in the spirit of truth. We must desire to be free, and then, we have to want to be kept by God. Any person who has truly sought the heart of God and has been delivered from ungodly soul ties will tell you there is a peace that surpasses all understanding that comes upon a person when they are free. There is an unspeakable joy that fills a person who is not bound by ungodly soul ties. People who aren't bound radiate a pure and unquestionable love that not only heals the brokenhearted, but it draws souls to Christ. Ministry isn't just speaking a bunch of religious words; ministry is demonstrating the Word of God in your life for others to see. There are so many liars in the pulpit these days, and because of this, the world no longer trusts the words of a preacher; they need to see demonstrations of power and love. How can we demonstrate the love and power of God if we ourselves are bound? The answer is simple: we can't.

Ask the Lord to free you from every ungodly soul tie you're in, and then, ask Him to give you an understanding regarding soul ties. Also ask Him to help you remain free. Please note that you still have to work at remaining free yourself. You can't walk into a lion's enclosure and expect the Lord to protect you if He hasn't told you to place yourself in that enclosure. You should never tempt the Lord, your God, meaning, you should never test God. He is not subject to you. Remember, faith without works is dead. Walk in the freedom that Christ Jesus's shed blood has afforded you and don't ever take that freedom for granted again. When you're free from all ungodly soul ties, every blessing God has for you can easily flow into your life, and every wrong thing that attempts to enter your life will be easily recognized. Be free, stay free and live free... that is God's desire for you. When God sends the people in your life who are appointed for your life, He will allow you to enter Godly soul ties with them, and that's when you'll better understand the God-ordained purposes of soul ties.

Printed in Great Britain
by Amazon

24272986R00178